# Irish politics today

**Politics Today**
Series editor: Bill Jones

Other titles in the series

# Irish politics today

*Third edition*

Neil Collins and Terry Cradden

Manchester University Press
Manchester and New York

*distributed exclusively in the USA by St. Martin's Press*

Copyright © Neil Collins and Frank McCann, 1989, 1991, 1997
and Terry Cradden 1997

First edition 1989
Second edition 1991, reprinted 1993

*Published by* Manchester University Press
Oxford Road, Manchester M13 9NR, UK
*and* Room 400, 175 Fifth Avenue, New York, NY 10010, USA

*Distributed exclusively in the USA by*
St. Martin's Press, Inc., 175 Fifth Avenue, New York,
NY 10010, USA

*British Library Cataloguing-in-Publication Data*
A catalogue record for this book is available from the British Library

*Library of Congress Cataloging-in-Publication Data*

Collins, Neil.
　　Irish politics today / Neil Collins and Terry Cradden. – 3rd ed.
　　　　p.　cm. – (Politics today)
　　ISBN 0-7190-5135-5 (C). – ISBN 0-7190-5136-3 (P)
　　　1. Ireland–Politics and government – 1949–　　I. Cradden, Terry.
　　II. Title.　III. Series: Politics today (Manchester, England)
　　JN1415.C66　1997
　　320.9415′09′049–dc21　　　　　　　　　　　　　　96–40139

ISBN　0 7190 5135 5 *hardback*
　　　0 7190 5136 3 *paperback*

First published 1997

01　00　99　98　97　　　　10　9　8　7　6　5　4　3　2　1

Typeset in Great Britain
by Servis Filmsetting Ltd, Manchester

Printed in Great Britain
by Bell & Bain Ltd, Glasgow

# Contents

# Tables

All figures have been rounded to the nearest whole number.

# Preface

A central message of this book, as it was of the two previous editions, is that Irish politics are too often presented as being so peculiar or *sui generis* as to defy 'standard' analyses. Ireland cannot be understood, according to some academic writers, by application of the theories and concepts which political scientists would apply elsewhere. Our contention, by contrast, is that the politics of Ireland *do* follow patterns similar to those found in other small states. The main difficulty with the former approach is that one gets little idea of whose interests routinely prevail in Irish politics. For example, in the distribution of resources – taxes, grants, permissions, restrictions and so on – who wins or loses? And why? Does policy favour some disproportionately; and actually ignore others? In this edition we have continued to try to discern the patterns of power as well as describe the mechanisms of politics.

The influence of Frank McCann, co-author of the first two editions, remains clear. We are indebted also to Paul Arthur, John Parr and Denise McLaughlin for practical assistance, advice, comments and queries. The content of politics changes very quickly, in Ireland as elsewhere; so we are grateful as well to numerous public servants, colleagues and students for their help in the updating of this book. Miriam and Margaret and our home-based children are, as always, due a special word of gratitude – for their much tested but enduring equanimity.

N.C., T.C.

# Abbreviations

| | |
|---|---|
| ATGWU | Amalgamated Transport and General Workers' Union (as the British TGWU is known in Ireland) |
| C &A-G | Comptroller and Auditor-General |
| CAP | Common Agricultural Policy |
| CFSP | Common Foreign and Security Policy |
| CIE | Coras Iompar Éireann (public transport authority) |
| CIU | Congress of Irish Unions |
| DED | Department of Economic Development (Northern Ireland) |
| DL | Democratic Left |
| DUP | Democratic Unionist Party |
| EMS | European Monetary System |
| EMU | Economic and Monetary Union |
| EPC | European Political Cooperation |
| ERDF | European Regional Development Fund |
| ERM | Exchange Rate Mechanism |
| ESB | Electricity Supply Board |
| EU | European Union |
| FWUI | Federated Workers Union of Ireland |
| ICMSA | Irish Creamery Milk Suppliers Association |
| ICTU | Irish Congress of Trade Unions |
| IDA | Industrial Development Authority |
| IFA | Irish Farmers Association |
| IGC | Intergovernmental Conference |
| IRA | Irish Republican Army |

| ITGWU  | Irish Transport and General Workers Union |
| ITUC   | Irish Trade Union Congress |
| LAC    | Local Appointments Commission |
| NATO   | North Atlantic Treaty Organisation |
| NESC   | National Economic and Social Council |
| NFA    | National Farmers Association |
| NICS   | Northern Ireland Civil Service |
| NIO    | Northern Ireland Office |
| PCW    | Programme for Competitiveness and Work |
| PDs    | Progressive Democrats |
| PESP   | Programme for Economic and Social Progress |
| PLAC   | Pro-Life Amendment Campaign |
| PNR    | Programme for National Recovery |
| PR     | Proportional Representation |
| PUP    | Progressive Unionist Party |
| RTE    | Radio Telefís Éireann |
| RUC    | Royal Ulster Constabulary |
| SDLP   | Social Democratic and Labour Party |
| SEA    | Single European Act |
| SF     | Sinn Féin |
| SFADCO | Shannon Free Airport Development Company |
| SIPTU  | Scientific, Industrial, Professional, Technical Union |
| SMI    | Strategic Management Initiative |
| SPUC   | Society for the Protection of the Unborn Child |
| STV    | Single Transferable Vote |
| TD     | Teachta Dála (Member of the Dáil) |
| UDA    | Ulster Defence Association |
| UDP    | Ulster Democratic Party |
| UKU    | United Kingdom Unionists |
| UUP    | Ulster Unionist Party |
| UVF    | Ulster Volunteer Force |
| WEU    | Western European Union |

# 1

# Ireland: what kind of state?

There are many aspects of life in Ireland that Irish people, as well as visitors to Ireland, regard as special and even unique. Politics in Ireland is no exception, for the Irish at home and abroad are a very political people. The story of Ireland is reflected in a rich tradition of literature, music, myth and involvement in politics. It is easy, therefore, to concentrate on what sets Ireland apart and to fail to see it in its wider context. Indeed, many books on Irish politics present a picture so full of scheming clerics, strange parties and manipulative politicians as to leave the reader more bemused than informed. Ireland, it seems, is always different.

In this chapter, we aim to put Ireland in its rightful and comprehensible place as an interesting example of a small, European, post-colonial, liberal-democratic, capitalist state, attempting to solve political problems of a kind common to other such countries, but in the light of its own particular conditions.

## Some historical background

The island of Ireland contains two jurisdictions: Northern Ireland, which is part of the United Kingdom, and the Republic of Ireland. The Republic, which for convenience is usually referred to as Ireland in this book, became politically independent from the UK in 1922, as the Irish Free State. It occupies twenty-six of the thirty-two counties into which the island was administratively divided when the treaty with Britain setting up the new state was signed.

The island of Ireland became inhabited comparatively recently. Until approximately 9,000 years ago it was apparently too cold to be attractive to humans. Since then, however, there have been invasions by several peoples – of whom the Celts were just one – and each of these incursions has had significant cultural and/or socio-political consequences. In political and institutional terms, Britain left the greatest legacy, reinforcing its grip on Ireland by the settling, or 'plantation', of English and Scottish Protestants loyal to the Crown on what was effectively confiscated land. The Tudor state stamped its authority firmly on the country by this means, and by 1603 English rule had superseded that of the Gaelic chiefs throughout most of the island. Despite periods of resistance, Ireland was subject to rule by Britain, in one form or another, until the years just before independence in the early 1920s.

Resistance to British rule was frequently influenced by developments abroad. When the Americans rebelled in the 1770s, Irish parliamentarians, their case buttressed by the existence of a military force of 'Volunteers', pressed for more legislative autonomy for Dublin. Again in 1789, the French Revolution encouraged the open organisation of agitation for parliamentary reform and national unity. What was to become a tradition of resistance by military means was reinforced in the 1798 Rebellion when, with the promise of French assistance, a Protestant radical named Wolfe Tone sought the subversion of British rule in Ireland. However, neither parliamentary nor military methods achieved the establishment of the more independent Irish political institutions being demanded – indeed the opposite was the case, for the existing Irish parliament, limited though its powers were, was soon to be abolished. Nor did these efforts achieve the greater unity of purpose between Catholics and Protestants, which was an ambition of the leadership of both forms of action; the '98 rebellion actually served to underline the separateness of the two religious groups.

The bulk of the native Irish population remained stubbornly

attached to Catholicism and were alienated from what was in effect the British Protestant state in Ireland. The Irish economy was regulated largely in the interests of Britain, which was itself in the process of becoming the world's most powerful capitalist country. By the mid-nineteenth century Ireland had a largely stock-rearing and cattle-exporting economy, and a steeply declining population. Deaths in the Famine in the years 1845-49 were about one million and a further 1.5 million people emigrated, mainly to Britain and the USA. By contrast, Britain's industrial revolution had made it a manufacturing giant. In Ireland, industry flourished only in the northeast where there was a Protestant settler majority.

---

**The Great Famine**

The population of Ireland almost doubled between 1800 and 1847. The 1841 census recorded a population of almost eight million. However, nearly one-third of the Irish were living at or below subsistence level, depending for their diet almost exclusively on the potato. The Great Famine resulted from the failure of the crop in successive years from 1845 to 1851. More than one million people died of starvation, and emigration reached massive proportions; by 1911, the Irish population had fallen to 4.4 million. The Great Famine had a major impact on Irish social structures, patterns of landholding and commerce. It also created a large and embittered American diaspora of Irish rural origin, for whom the British were the guilty party in not providing sufficient food and other economic aid to prevent the tragedy.

---

The Act of Union of 1800 was intended to bind Ireland more closely to Britain; so while many state functions continued to be administered in Dublin, from then on Ireland was governed from London, with a senior Cabinet Minister as Irish Chief Secretary. Irish constituencies returned members to the parliament at

Westminster on a franchise similar to that in England. Throughout the nineteenth century, modern democratic institutions such as disciplined parliamentary groupings and mass party organisation also developed in Ireland, principally during the periods of political leadership of Daniel O'Connell and Charles Stewart Parnell. In the early part of the century, O'Connell focused on the repeal of the 'Penal' laws which forced Catholics into an inferior social, political and economic position. Later on Parnell took up the issues of land reform and Home Rule. Both set new standards in political oratory and in astute parliamentary manoeuvring. Although neither achieved all of his objectives, they laid the foundations of popular respect in Ireland for parliamentary democracy. Their legacy survives in the primary place given to parliamentary institutions and to parliamentary methods by Irish political leaders down to the present day.

---

**Home Rule**

'Home Rule' was shorthand for the restoration to Ireland of a parliament, subordinate in certain respects to the British government, but with general autonomy over domestic legislation. From 1870 onwards it became the main rallying call for those Irish hostile to British rule. Two Home Rule Bills, intended to give Ireland limited self-government within the Empire, were defeated in the UK parliament in the late nineteenth century. The Third Home Rule Bill, introduced by Asquith's Liberal government, was eventually passed in 1914; but it was never to take effect.

---

By the end of the nineteenth century also, a system of local government and a public service based on the new British principle of recruitment on merit – rather than by social rank or influence – were well established in Ireland. By the first decade of the twentieth century the Irish were enjoying the same or similar levels of welfare, educational and property rights as other UK subjects. Only in the most senior public positions was the Anglo-Irish Protestant elite still firmly entrenched.

### Independence

By the 1890s century popular sentiment for what was called 'Home Rule' was expressed mainly through the Irish Parliamentary Party, which held the great majority of the parliamentary seats in Ireland. Using its numerical strength and the pivotal voting role that this gave it in a British parliament split between Conservatives and Liberals, the Irish Party eventually managed to secure a Home Rule Act, in September 1914. However, the First World War had begun in August and the implementation the Act was postponed for the duration of hostilities. Partly as a consequence, the initiative in the campaign for some form of independence passed out of the hands of the parliamentarians.

---

#### '1916' – The Easter Rising

The Easter Rising of April 1916 marked the beginning of the military campaign for independence. The rising was an initial failure involving about 2,000 insurrectionists, mainly in Dublin. A few hundred people were killed and much damage done in Dublin city centre. Public reaction, as far as can be judged by contemporary Dublin papers, was initially hostile. It began to favour the militants following the execution of their leaders and the internment of many others. At the 1918 general election, militants, under the banner of Sinn Féin, routed the more moderate Irish Party. Though now subject to more critical historical analysis, the 1916 Easter Rising has a major symbolic importance in Ireland. The 'heroic failure' is still seen by many Nationalists as the 'blood sacrifice' that was necessary to reawaken the Irish to a sense of their nationhood.

---

Remarkably, it was as a consequence of the failure of an armed republican revolt that the much less prevalent militaristic tradition of Irish nationalism gained the upper hand. The execution by the British authorities of the leaders of the Easter Rising in 1916 had several effects: it produced an angry public mood at what was seen to be a disproportionately punitive response; it gave retrospective justification for the resort to arms; and it provided a legitimation for later episodes of 'armed struggle'. Thus when the Great War ended Britain found itself dealing with much more radical and militant politicians.

Their party, Sinn Féin, rejected Home Rule, demanded total independence from Britain, and won an overwhelming majority of Irish seats at the 1918 British general election. Rather than present themselves at Westminster, in 1919 the Sinn Féin MPs formed their own parliament in Dublin, Dáil Eireann, which became the effective political arm of the militant independence movement. The British sought unsuccessfully to suppress it by force of arms; but by 1921, with both parties weary of the struggle, it ended with Partition – a negotiated division of Ireland into the Irish Free State and Northern Ireland (see Chapter 7). This Anglo-Irish Treaty of 1921 had a decisive effect on the development of Irish politics. As will be seen in more detail in Chapter 3, Sinn Féin split over the Treaty, and a bitter civil war between the opposing sides followed. The roots of what are still the two main political parties in Ireland can be traced to this: Fianna Fáil, which emerged from the anti-Treaty tradition; and Fine Gael with a pro-Treaty lineage.

### Political institutions and the Constitution

The political institutions of Ireland, which will be examined in more detail in subsequent chapters, are – for the most part – based on the Westminster model. Indeed, because of the wide range of functions devolved to the Chief Secretary's Office in Dublin Castle, the Irish Free State inherited an almost complete administrative apparatus, together with other important state institutions, at its formation in 1922. It thus had little difficulty in grafting on new ones to cope with tasks, like defence and foreign affairs, which had formerly been reserved to London. Compared with many other newly independent states, therefore, at this institutional level in particular, Ireland enjoyed a fairly smooth transition.

The Constitution of the Free State was replaced in 1937, although there was considerable continuity with the previous one. The architect of the new Constitution, Bunreacht na hEireann – which remains in force – was the then Taoiseach (Prime Minister), Eamonn de Valera, the leader of Fianna Fáil and former chief of the anti-Treaty forces in the civil war.

---

**The main features of Bunreacht na hEireann – the Constitution**

- *The republican nature of the state*: an elected but non-executive President as head (although the Republic was not formally declared until 1948).
- *The unitary nature of the state*: the State Parliament is the supreme law-making body, though it must not enact laws repugnant to the Constitution – and has, since 1973, had to take account also of European Union obligations.
- *The separation of powers*: the organs of government are divided into executive, legislative and judicial, each with limited and distinct functions.
- *A bicameral (two-chamber) legislature*: the Oireachtas, composed of an upper house, Seanad Eireann (the Senate), and a lower house, Dáil Eireann, together with the President.
- *A government*: to carry out executive functions within the constraints of the Constitution and the law.
- *Independent courts*: which incorporate the judicial power; the court of final appeal is called the Supreme Court.

Each of the institutions referred to in the Constitution – presidency, Oireachtas, government and courts – is given specific powers, to be exercised in accordance with the general principles of a British-style parliamentary democracy (although the Constitution does have some non-British features such as judicial review). In contrast with Britain, the fact that the Constitution is written means that governments and legislators must take particular care to act within its provisions. On the other hand, some of these are very general, and thus quite difficult to interpret; for example, many of them reflect the social thinking of the mid-1930s, especially that of the Catholic Church. (Article 44, deleted in 1974, actually recognised the 'special position' of the Roman Catholic Church as the church of the majority of the state's citizens.)

Furthermore, some important conventions are not stated explicitly; for example, political parties are not formally recognised. In any case, the courts are the final arbiters of what is or is not constitutional; and the only method of altering the Constitution is by a referendum of the people.

Given the changing social structure of Ireland, it seems likely that the Constitution and the system of law associated with it will change at an accelerating rate over the next few years. The Constitution specifically allows for continuity of previous statutes and the British common law tradition, provided these are not inconsistent with its own provisions. Such inconsistencies have occasionally arisen, and there was formerly a tendency for Irish legislators and judges to look to Britain for ideas on statute and precedent. Recently, however, there has been a greater willingness to be innovative, particularly by judges. Irish politics today are thus becoming less 'British', as politicians, bureaucrats and jurists reflect the experience of three-quarters of a century of self-government, and of a great deal more contact with the wider world.

A particular boost to this process of change, especially in economic terms, has been provided by Ireland's membership of the European Union (EU) and its predecessor bodies.[1] As will be outlined in later chapters, the EU and its governing treaties introduced an important new source of policies, laws and court rulings into Irish politics. Beyond institutional influences, Ireland has also increased its openness to change through a deliberate expansion of its trading relations, mainly with Europe but also with the rest of the world.

## The Irish economy before independence

Until the Act of Union, Ireland's own parliament had at least some powers to regulate trade. Under the Union, with a single parliament at Westminster, the two islands became, for most purposes, a free trade area. Although several Irish industries – leather, silk, glass, hardware, furniture and wool – were permitted to retain the protection of an import tariff for a time, by 1824 all duties between Ireland and Britain had been abolished. Ireland, with what then appeared to be a lack of the raw materials necessary for industrial and economic take-off, was tied to open trading with an area experiencing huge economic growth; this put it at a great disadvantage compared with most of the rest of the UK.

It remained economically underdeveloped for the greater part of the nineteenth century, therefore, with the majority of its population dependent on a subsistence agriculture. Ireland was, as the Famine demonstrated, extremely vulnerable to the vagaries of nature as well as to the laws of the market. At the beginning of the twentieth century the main characteristic of the Irish economy remained its dependence on agriculture and, more particularly, the export of live cattle to Britain. By the outbreak of the First World War Ireland enjoyed an almost monopoly position in supplying the British market with agricultural produce.

## The economy after independence

It lay at the core of the case of the advocates of Irish independence that economic underdevelopment, and the resulting poverty and emigration, were the outcome of deliberate government policy. Although deprived of the relatively more prosperous and industrialised northeast of Ireland as a consequence of the Treaty, therefore, one of the greatest challenges facing the Free State was to improve the performance of its economy.

---

**Ireland in the world economy – the three zone model**

- The *core* zone – the 'First World' – is made up of countries like Britain, Germany, Japan and the USA, and it is here that much of the wealth of the world is concentrated.
- The *periphery* is made up of the countries known as the 'Third World'. The core relies upon the periphery for many industrial raw materials, and for some of its food. The countries of the periphery are usually dependent on mineral production or a single food crop for their export earnings.
- The *semi-periphery* countries are intermediate in status. They have a more diversified economic structure, and industrialisation is often well advanced. Much industry is locally owned, and wage rates and living standards are significantly higher than in the periphery. Peripheral countries often become semi-peripheral by reliance on investment by multinationals – which will be attracted by the availability of an educated and skilled workforce; a developed infrastructure – roads and telecommunications; lower wage rates than in the core; and financial inducements from government.

This model helps us to understand Ireland's position – as a small, but relatively advanced, semi-peripheral, liberal-capitalist state, with a still significant agricultural sector.

---

The first problem to be tackled was that agricultural exports had declined sharply after the First World War, in the face of increased competition from Denmark, New Zealand and elsewhere. The new government took immediate action to help recover export markets, especially those in Britain, and the short term results were impressive. The export of dairy produce increased dramatically, as did the overall value of agricultural exports. However, world events militated against the maintenance of the improvement.

As a key international player, Britain underwent a severe economic crisis in the late 1920s following the collapse in global financial markets. The UK government reacted by erecting barriers against imports into Britain, and by the early 1930s a general tariff on all imports had been introduced. Access to the UK market was also restricted by other government measures affecting food products, introduced in the interests of its own farmers. Ireland was obviously affected by the general world recession also, and although the governing party, Cumann na nGaedheal (the predecessor of Fine Gael), was generally in favour of free trade, it too imposed tariffs on food imports.

## Protectionism

A change of government in 1932 brought a more determined move away from free trade, and towards protectionism. This reorientation had a political as well as an economic basis. De Valera, the leader of the new government party, Fianna Fáil, had a particular vision of Ireland, expressed most clearly in a famous radio broadcast made on St Patrick's Day in 1943:

> That Ireland, which we dreamed of, would be the home of a people who valued material wealth as the basis of right living, of a people who were satisfied with frugal comfort and devoted their leisure to the things of the spirit – a land whose countryside would be bright with cosy homesteads, whose fields and villages would be joyous with the sound of industry, with the romping of sturdy children, the contest of athletic youths and the laughter of comely maidens, whose firesides would be forums for the wisdom of serene old age. It would, in a word, be the home of a people living the life that God desires that man should live.[2]

Plainly in keeping with this vision, Fianna Fáil had developed a policy of economic self-sufficiency. This was to be achieved by the

protection by tariffs of the home market, thereby giving existing
domestic producers a better chance of surviving, and providing
incentives to encourage the establishment of new indigenous
industrial enterprises. Under the previous government a producer had had to argue a case *for* protection; under the new dis-
pensation protection was to be given unless a case could be made
*against* it. Giving effect to this, the 1932 Emergency Imposition
of Duties Act gave the government wide powers to impose, vary
or revoke customs duties as and when it wished. Within a few
months Ireland became one of the most heavily protected
markets in the world; by 1937 imports of some 1,947 different
items were controlled by this means.

Nevertheless, the late 1930s brought renewed difficulties for
Irish farmers, all the more so as the government tried to diversify
production behind trade barriers. A system of guaranteed prices
with restrictions on imports brought an emphasis on food crops
for home consumption, but decline had set in. To add to these
problems there was a short but acrimonious dispute known as
'the economic war', sparked by the Irish government's refusal to
pass on land annuities (essentially mortgage payments) owed to
Britain by farmers who had bought property using government
loans under the Land Acts of the nineteenth century. Fianna
Fáil's case was that these payments were imperialistic, and
demeaning to Ireland and its people. Britain responded by
increasing tariffs on Irish exports to the UK; the Irish, in turn,
erected similar barriers against British goods entering Ireland.

The row finally ended in 1938 with a general agreement on
reducing tariffs between the two countries and – a curious
concession given the rumbling intimations of trouble to come
from Hitler's Germany – the handing into Irish control of the
naval facilities (or 'Treaty Ports') which Britain had retained in
Ireland under the 1921 Treaty.

### The Second World War

Although the Free State was largely preoccupied by affairs
within its own boundaries during the early years of its existence,

the ending of Partition remained on the agenda of all political parties in the state. Fianna Fáil took a particularly strident anti-Partition view, and de Valera insisted that neutrality in the Second World War was his government's only possible option for so long as Ireland remained divided. Although formally neutral, however, and publicly vilified in Britain for this stance, Ireland clearly 'leaned' towards the Anglo-American Alliance. Exports to the UK continued throughout the war, and much evidence has accumulated of covert activities in Ireland of benefit only to the Allied side.[3]

Access to food imports from abroad was clearly restricted during the course of the war, so there was a substantial increase in the production of crops purely for home consumption. As a result, acres under tillage were vastly increased, while the output of livestock and livestock products obviously fell as access to export markets diminished. After the war, with financial aid under the USA's Marshall Plan, Europe set about rebuilding its shattered economies. Not unexpectedly, it was decided that Ireland's main contribution to European recovery would be in the production of food for export. The official economic planning programme for the period 1949-53 accepted this as the primary policy.

## Agricultural uncertainty

Agriculture thus remained the principal economic activity in Ireland, and although it has declined quite sharply in recent years, it is still a major contributor. In the early 1990s agriculture contributed around 20 per cent to merchandise exports, accounted for more than 10 per cent of gross national product, and provided approximately one-sixth of total employment. (In the EU as a whole, agriculture by then contributed 4 per cent to GNP and provided 8 per cent of employment.) But all this masks the huge underlying changes in Irish farming since the end of the Second World War.

Successive governments maintained Ireland's essentially protectionist fiscal regime until the early 1960s, when it seemed that Ireland would soon be a member of the EU and be obliged to open up all of its protected industry to competition. In the event, the entry of the UK and Ireland was delayed until 1973; but by then, under an Anglo-Irish agreement of 1966, they were already operating in an almost tariff-free environment between themselves. Before 1973, however, the European Common Agricultural Policy (CAP) had virtually closed EU markets to Irish cattle and beef; Ireland's membership was to change all that:

> The principal aspirations of post-war agricultural policy have been largely met by Ireland's accession to the E[U]. The original emphasis in the CAP on security of food supply has provided access for Irish agricultural products to a large market, with the bonus of price guarantees for certain major products.[4]

Farming enjoyed particular prosperity between 1970 and 1978, as over-reliance on the British market decreased. Agricultural output rose at almost 4 per cent per annum, the highest recorded rate of prolonged growth, and efficiency increased dramatically through the application of new technology and improved managerial skills But since the late 1970s Irish agriculture has experienced fluctuating fortunes, and has suffered much greater uncertainty. Moreover, the future is now largely outside the control of Irish governments: through its price support mechanisms and management of the market, the CAP influences and largely determines the conditions under which Irish farm output is produced and sold.[5]

Further, the future of the CAP is itself in doubt. It has come under frequent attack as a grossly inefficient and highly expensive way of maintaining farm employment. Accusations of feather-bedding and fraud abound, and the 'mountains' and 'lakes' of unsold produce, to which Irish beef and dairy products once contributed, were argued to be wasteful, even immoral. Whether the CAP remains in place in its present form or not, what seems likely to continue is the process by which some Irish farms become larger, more efficient and commercially run, while many will remain small, inefficient and unable to sustain their owners without substantial government and EU help. De Valera's dream of a rural Ireland made up mainly of small family farms, worked by their owners, has been eroded by world market conditions.

## Foreign investment, industrialisation and employment

The Republic of Ireland's move from protection to free trade was a result of more than just the change in world conditions. The 1950s were years of increasing economic difficulty and political uncertainty. Multi-party coalition governments, led by Fine Gael, had been no more successful in solving these problems than had Fianna Fáil, so continuing unemployment, poverty and emigration put all parties under considerable pressure to rethink their economic approach. Protectionism and self-sufficiency had been tried; and while successful in creating an industrial base where none existed before, they were plainly now failing to meet the needs of the people of Ireland. Although begun to be developed under a coalition government, the new approach which eventually emerged has come to be particularly identified with the advent of Sean Lemass to the leadership of Fianna Fáil. A vastly experienced minister and skilled but pragmatic political operator, he succeeded de Valera in 1959.

The essential thrust of the new policy was to open up the Irish economy to foreign capital. As well as the decline in agricultural employment, it was also becoming clear that the industries protected by tariffs and quotas were often, in the absence of competition, inefficient and complacent – and they had patently failed to absorb the loss of employment on the land. A central prop of the new policy was to increase industrial development by encouraging multinational firms to set up in Ireland. Such foreign investment, it was hoped, would increase employment, expand the domestic market, improve the balance of payments by way of exports, and create opportunities for new Irish businesses to serve some of the needs of the multinationals.

The initial achievements of the new policy certainly seemed impressive. Foreign-owned firms provided 22,000 new jobs between 1973 and 1980 alone; and they presently employ around 90,000 people – over a third of the manufacturing workforce. On the other hand, Ireland has not quite become a 'core' economy. New jobs have often been unskilled or semi-skilled, in operations involving the importation of expensive components from elsewhere purely for assembly in Ireland. In other cases the manufacturing processes have been too capital-intensive to reduce unemployment as much as was hoped – in other words, the average cost of each new job created has been too high. And not enough foreign firms have located in the poorer regions.

### A harsher future?

There have been other depressing signs. In the face of economic 'globalisation', Irish wage rates began to look uncompetitive in the 1990s, and the 'social costs' of employment – sickness, pensions, unemployment and other welfare benefits – were also very high by world standards. As a consequence, multinational companies closed down previously successful Irish assembly operations, and moved production to what might be called 'new' semi-peripheral countries, where low labour and social costs are the main attraction. Even some native Irish companies began to 'out-source' production to former Communist countries in eastern Europe. There were, at the same time, some positive developments, particularly in the electronics, information services and computer software sectors, where young Irish graduates are now being employed in increasing numbers. Also interesting has been the blooming of home-grown, Irish-based multinationals – in the paper and packaging, building products, food processing, banking and newspaper sectors.

It is clear, therefore, that the industrial sector of the Irish economy has been making a greatly increased contribution to the wealth of the country; and industry's share of gross domestic product has more than made up for the decline of the agriculture sector. But industrial employment has failed to keep pace with the increasing number of young people arriving on the labour market; some well qualified men and women still have to emigrate if they wish to fulfil their potential. It seems fair to say, therefore, that Ireland's 'new' industrial strategy has not entirely lived up to expectations.

## EU regional policy

Where market forces alone are permitted to determine the location of industry and commerce, wealth will tend to be centred in fewer and fewer locations. Until accession to the EU, Irish governments occasionally sought, albeit in piecemeal fashion, to attend to the lack of economic activity in particular regions, but with uneven success. In an effort to tackle the problem of regional imbalance Europe-wide, the six original members of the EU agreed to set a ceiling on the amount of government assistance for investment projects in the more prosperous regions. Following enlargement and the accession of Ireland and Britain, the system of ceilings was extended, and the regions of Europe were divided into four groups. In the first were the rich regions, where the original ceiling continued to apply. The fourth group was formed of the poorest regions, including both Northern Ireland and the Republic, to which no ceiling applied – so long as other EU requirements were not breached. And to provide additional aid for these poorer regions, the European Regional Development Fund (ERDF) was established.

But the fact that the whole of the Republic was included among the poorer regions meant that much of the ERDF money, and other so-called 'structural' funding, was spent in relatively developed parts of the country, leaving those areas which have always been starved of industry and investment not much better off than before. In the context of the 1992 Single Market and the Maastricht Treaty, some effort is being made to address the so far unattended development needs of the poorer regions. 'Cohesion' funding, intended to ensure a more equal sharing of economic opportunity, is now flowing, and the Irish countryside is dotted with signs marking projects funded by the EU. However, the expected accession to the EU of other much less developed semi-periphery countries is bound to mean less and less support for

Irish industrial and infrastructural development as we approach the end of the twentieth century.

### The Irish language

Irish is, under the terms of Bunreacht na hEireann, the 'first national language', and the Constitution recognises English purely as a second official language. However, Irish is spoken as a first language only in areas known as the Gaeltacht, situated mainly along the western seaboard, and official efforts to have it more widely used have, by and large, been a failure. According to the most recent census there are more than one million Irish speakers in the Republic. This figure, 31.6 per cent of the population, is in fact a vast overestimate of the numbers who can speak Irish competently, and actually use it regularly. The language remains an important part of Irish culture, nevertheless, and many non-Irish speakers support attempts to safeguard its place in education, broadcasting and official business. Indeed, several national agencies exist to encourage and preserve the use of the language – although the Constitutional Review Group, which reported in 1996, called for English to be recognised as of equal status as an official language.

### The European Monetary System

Even after independence Ireland's currency remained linked to sterling, leaving monetary policy to be decided entirely by Britain. What had been a fairly satisfactory arrangement, however, began to be a problem when Ireland imported, perforce, the high British inflation rates of the 1970s. As the result of a controversial decision in 1979, the direct link with sterling finally ended. Soon after, the Irish pound (or punt) became part of the Exchange Rate Mechanism (ERM) of the putative European Monetary System (EMS). This development had patently beneficial effects as regards inflation, but it also decreased the ability of Irish governments to resist the movement of wealth to European core countries. Moreover, a significant amount of Ireland's trade remains with the UK, and Britain's failure to keep the pound sterling within the ERM means that there is still significant exchange rate uncertainty.

For example, while for many years the Irish pound ran fairly steadily at a value just below that of sterling, by the early 1990s the reverse became the case, causing obvious difficulties for Irish exporters. The EMS aptly demonstrates the limits to the 'independence' of a small country on the periphery of a market whose riches tend to be concentrated in the centre.

## Conclusion

On the face of it, it is surely remarkable that the Republic of Ireland should be among the most stable states in Europe. However, in essence this is because of the values passed down by the political actors who led the Irish independence movement. One of the strongest influences on this elite was the parliamentary tradition. Even when the more militant independence movement developed early this century, its instincts remained fundamentally parliamentarian. The parliamentary tradition was all the stronger because its roots lay in the ideals of the American and French revolutions: that power resides in the people and is only exercised on their behalf by elected representatives. It is also important to note that independence was achieved without the intervention of other major powers. This made the post-independence period in Ireland less violent than in many other countries. The final factor making for stability was the ease with which power was transferred; and one of the main reasons for this was the vital continuity of so many political and administrative institutions.

Unlike many other countries which have become independent in the twentieth century, then, the Republic of Ireland has remained a stable liberal democracy with fair and competitive elections, alternating parties in government, an independent judiciary and unchallenged civilian control of the military. It also enjoys a vigorous and variegated free press, and broadcasting services of high journalistic as well as technical standards. What is perhaps a less understandable difference between Irish politics and those in many, if not most, other European countries is the absence of a left–right divide – and in particular that the main democratic socialist party, also the oldest party in Ireland, has enjoyed only intermittent success at the polls. This question is addressed in Chapter 3.

There were serious deficiencies in economic policy during the early history of the state, and major economic challenges remain to be responded to; with almost half of Ireland's population under the age of twenty-five, it could hardly be otherwise. But while it is not yet among the most wealthy countries of Europe, Ireland remains close to the top of the world league as regards the incomes of its citizens. The Irish also enjoy health and welfare services, housing and education – not to mention a natural environment – of an enviably high quality by international standards. Economic growth levels in 1996 were higher than the EU average, and Ireland was also running a substantial balance of payments surplus. One writer has recently argued that by reference to every significant economic and social indicator, Ireland is now part of the 'First World'.[6]

The other side of the coin is that economic success brings new problems, of a kind virtually unheard of only a very few years ago. Although Ireland is, statistically at any rate, the most law-abiding country in Europe,[7] in Dublin and other urban centres there has been what some have described as a 'crime epidemic' since the 1980s. This has been manifest in a variety of forms, ranging from youthful drug abuse, domestic burglaries and 'joyriding' in stolen cars, through to Mafia-style organised crime: armed robberies, protection rackets and 'contract killings' – including, it would appear, the gunning down in June 1996 of a well known investigative journalist as she drove home from a court hearing.

Overlaid on this 'ordinary' crime, there is much evidence of the involvement in criminal activities of the Irish Republican

Army (IRA) and other fringe republican paramilitary groups. Robberies to fund the purchase of arms, and to defray other 'expenses' of the armed struggle, have featured in Irish crime statistics since the early 1970s. Particular public revulsion was engendered by the shooting dead of a Garda (police) officer in the course of a raid by a 'rogue' IRA unit on a vehicle delivering cash to post offices in the Limerick area in mid-1996. Paradoxically perhaps, another role of the paramilitaries has been as self-righteous vigilantes dispensing very rough justice indeed to Dublin city drug dealers. All this reminds us of the potentially most disruptive influence on Irish politics today: Northern Ireland, the major unresolved question of the 1922 settlement (see Chapter 7).

## Notes

1 The European Union was initially called the European Economic Community, and later simply the European Community; to avoid confusion all references hereafter will be to the 'European Union' or the 'EU'.
2 M. Moynihan (ed.), *Speeches and Statements of de Valera*, Dublin: Gill & Macmillan, 1980, pp. 466-9.
3 See, for example, Robert Fisk, *In Time of War*, London: Paladin, 1985.
4 Sean Dooney, *Irish Agriculture*, Dublin: Institute of Public Administration, 1988, p. 6.
5 *Ibid., p.* 6.
6 Liam Kennedy, *Colonialism, Religion and Nationalism in Ireland*, Belfast: Queen's University Institute of Irish Studies, 1996. Some confirmation of this can be found in a recent United Nations report, which shows Ireland to be in nineteenth place in the UN's World Development Index – which reflects, in particular, life expectancy, education and income (cited in *The Irish Times*, 16 July 1996).
7 As regards its crime rate, Ireland is also fourth lowest among reporting nations in a world survey conducted by the UN (*ibid.*).

## Further reading

P. Bew, E. Hazelkorn and H. Patterson, *The Dynamics of Irish Politics*, London: Lawrence & Wishart, 1989

T. Brown, *Ireland: a Social and Cultural History 1922-1979*, Glasgow: Fontana, 1982.

J. Coakley and M. Gallagher (eds), *Politics in the Republic of Ireland*, Dublin: Folens, 1993.

R. Foster, *Modern Ireland 1600-1972*, London: Allen Lane, 1988.

B. Girvin, *Between Two Worlds: Politics and Economy in Independent Ireland*, Dublin: Gill & Macmillan, 1989.

K. Kennedy, T. Giblin and D. McHugh, *The Economic Development of Ireland in the Twentieth Century*, London: Routledge, 1988.

J. Lee, *Ireland 1912-1985, Politics and Society*, Cambridge: Cambridge University Press, 1989.

# 2

# Parties, elections and electorates

Virtually all liberal democracies have competing political parties, and in most European countries these parties are based on social distinctions or cleavages. Within the Republic of Ireland, however, the party system reflects no obvious social divisions; Ireland is similar to the USA in that the main parties stand principally on their records rather than their position on an ideological spectrum.

Before independence there were two distinct groups on the island, differentiated by culture, religion, language and class. This division was reflected in the different attitudes of the two groups to the 'national question'. To understand the development of the present Irish party system, we must examine how the struggle for national independence became dominated largely by the Catholic, Gaelic Irish.

## The Protestant ascendancy

The plantations involved the replacement of the native Irish in positions of economic and political power by people relocated from Britain. The massive changes in the ownership of land caused by the plantations have been an enduring cause of social bitterness and political dissent right up to the present day. Along with the policy of plantation, attempts were made to integrate the Irish forcibly into a more English way of life. The British government sought to suppress the Gaelic language and culture, as well as the Catholic religion. This naturally created great animosity between the Irish and those they regarded as invaders. The conflict between planters and natives was further exacerbated by the struggle for the British Crown between the Protestant forces of William of Orange and the Catholic armies of James II. William's victory at the Battle of the Boyne in 1690 ensured Protestant ascendancy in Ireland.

## Catholic emancipation and the rise of nationalism

The struggle for Catholic emancipation reached its peak in 1829 when the rights of Catholics to vote and to sit in the parliament at Westminster were finally secured. Despite these political gains, however, Catholic disaffection with British rule continued. As we have already noted, their economic problems were exacerbated by integration with Britain, and the Great Famine was but the most dramatic manifestation of this.

Farm ownership became a key issue, and eventual success on this score was a consequence of a period of intense agitation led by radical nationalists against the Protestant landowning class. Nationalism and Catholicism thus became synonymous at grass-roots level. For Catholics, it became clear that Ireland must have its own parliament, with the ability to regulate its trade with Britain, if it was to develop economically. But although Irish Catholics were a very small group in the UK parliament, Irish Protestants were only too aware that they would be swamped in any future Irish parliament by Catholic members.

The difference in attitudes to British rule between the Protestants, mostly concentrated in the northeast, and the great majority of the rest of the population was eventually to be expressed in the shape of new Irish political parties. The general election of 1868 was the last in Ireland to be dominated by the English party labels of Liberal and Conservative. By 1885 only two parties took seats in Ireland: the nationalist Irish Party, led by Parnell, with a strategy of offering support to whichever English party would help the Irish claim for its own parliament; and the Unionists, whose sole objective was to prevent Home

Rule. This remained the position until the 1919 general election.

By then, arguably as a direct consequence of the execution of the leaders of the 1916 Easter Rising by the British, Sinn Féin had won nationalist sympathies from Home Rule within the UK to the creation of an independent Irish republic. Sinn Féin's overwhelming victory in the election led to the setting up of Dáil Eireann. The British government proscribed the Dáil in September 1919 and arrested some of its members, but it continued to meet in secret.

## The War of Independence

For the next few years a guerrilla campaign or 'War of Independence' was waged against the British in Ireland. In May 1921 general elections were called for the two parliaments set up by the Government of Ireland Act 1920. But while some battle was done in Northern Ireland, in the south not one seat was uncontested. Sinn Féin took 124 and the remaining 4, the university seats, went to independents from Trinity College Dublin. This result strengthened the resolve of the nationalists, and obviously undermined Britain's position. In July 1921 the War of Independence came to an end with the Anglo-Irish Treaty.

## The Civil War

The Treaty divided Sinn Féin. Those who agreed with it believed it was the most that could be won at that time – and that it laid the basis for eventually securing an independent all-Ireland state. The Treaty was passed by the Dáil, after an acrimonious debate, by 64 votes to 57. A further general election was held in 1922 and the result was a clear majority for acceptance of the Treaty – the anti-Treatyites won only 36 out of 128 seats. Twelve days after the election civil war broke out between the opposing sides. More than 600 lives were lost, and the Civil War created divided loyalties and animosities which were to last for decades. It ended in May 1923 when the anti-Treaty forces laid down their arms, but refused to accept the legitimacy of the government or the state. Although the division of Sinn Féin over the Treaty, and the Civil War that resulted, provided the basis for the party system in the Free State, as we shall see, the Civil War 'split' itself reflects older divisions.

## The breakup of Sinn Féin

In April 1923 the pro-Treaty deputies in Dáil Eireann organised themselves into a new party, Cumann na nGaedheal (League of the Gaels). Membership was open to anyone who supported the Treaty and the new Constitution. Remarkably perhaps, given earlier evidence of public support for the Treaty, at the general election of August 1923 Cumann na nGaedheal won only 39 per cent of the total vote, giving it sixty-three seats. The anti-Treatyites, or Republicans – reorganised by de Valera to fight the election as 'Sinn Féin' – won 27.4 per cent, and forty-four seats. Sinn Féin's electoral programme consisted of an outright refusal to sit in the Dáil or to accept the Free State.

## A hint of class division?

Before examining the birth and rise of Fianna Fáil, which was to become the major force in Irish politics for many decades, we should pause to examine the influence of social cleavage on the early party system in the Free State. The system had been dominated since the 1880s by the demand for legislative independence from Britain. Catholics, who had suffered most under British rule, supported independence. The effect of the separatist struggle was to create a Catholic cross-class alliance; but latent class divisions were to become more obvious in the divide within the nationalist camp over the Treaty. In general, it was supported by those groups who had most to gain from continued links with the British Commonwealth – the larger business owners, the merchants and 'big' farmers. The Treaty preserved trade links with Britain, and served to bolster their economic and political position within Ireland. These groups supported Cumann na nGaedheal which, in government between 1923 and 1932, followed a policy of free trade intended to protect Ireland's markets in Britain. In 1926, 97 per cent of Irish exports went to the UK (including Northern Ireland); and 76 per cent of imports came from the UK.

Landless farmers and farm labourers, on the other hand, gave their support to the anti-Treaty side. In part this was because they shared the long term aim of making Ireland economically self-sufficient. Such a policy would involve maintaining price supports for agricultural products – in much the same way that the EU does today – thus guaranteeing the incomes of small producers. The second, and major, plank in the 'self-sufficiency' strategy was industrial development. This too was to be achieved by protecting the domestic market from overseas competition. Protectionism inevitably attracted the support of small business people, whose firms stood a greater chance of survival when shielded against the availability of lower-priced goods from overseas. Indeed, protectionism also won the support of industrial workers, because of the increased employment opportunities which it promised. Thus the Civil War division did have some social basis, and the emergence of Fianna Fáil confirmed this very clearly.

### The rise of Fianna Fáil

The anti-Treaty leader, de Valera, resigned from Sinn Féin and founded a new party, Fianna Fáil (The Soldiers of Destiny), in 1926. In the general election of June 1927, Fianna Fáil won forty-four seats, while the remnants of Sinn Féin (which followed a policy of not taking its seats in the Dáil) won only five. By contrast with Cumann na nGaedheal, the party in government, Fianna Fáil claimed most of its support from the less well-off sections of Irish society, and it expended much effort on building up a strong organisation based on constituency (called *cumainn:* party clubs). Further, Fianna Fáil developed policies that seemed more attuned to Ireland's needs after the worldwide economic crisis of the late 1920s. In particular, Fianna Fáil argued for protecting the domestic market.

At the general election in 1932, Fianna Fáil increased its vote by almost 10 per cent and formed a minority government with support from the Labour Party. It made further gains in 1933, enabling it to remain in office in its own right; and there it stayed for an unbroken run until 1948. As the sole party of government for this lengthy period, it was able to consolidate and extend its basis of support. Firstly, through its attachment to protectionism and the economic strategy of self-sufficiency, Fianna Fáil won support from the business community, from farmers (at the expense of Cumann na nGaedheal). Secondly, by the introduction of new welfare measures, particularly the introduction of unemployment benefit, it also won over much of the urban working class (at the expense of Labour, as we shall see). In these years, therefore, Fianna Fáil developed into a classic 'catch-all' party, drawing its support from almost all sections of Irish society.

### 'Labour must wait'

The Irish Labour Party is the oldest party presently operating in the Republic of Ireland, having been formed as a wing of the trade union movement during the First World War. Moreover, much of its early inspiration came from one of Europe's most impressive self-taught Marxist thinkers, James Connolly – who was executed for his part in the Easter Rising. But Labour has enjoyed only intermittent success with the voters. De Valera was himself sure that Irish politics would eventually conform to a typically European class-based model. However, he was also convinced that this would not happen until the national question had been settled once and for all; thus his famous remark that 'Labour must wait.'

Why has Ireland been different in this important respect? In part it was because of the homogeneity of its social structure for, to begin with at any rate, the cleavages which did exist were comparatively slight. The difference also had much to do with the timing and result of the struggle for independence, which took place when the country was industrially underdeveloped, and thus possessed a relatively small industrial proletariat – the natural constituency for a party of labour. Further, the industrial heartland of the island, Belfast and the Lagan Valley, was severed from the rest of the country by the Government of Ireland Act 1920. In addition, the Land Acts of the late nineteenth century which permitted farmers to buy their farms, produced a very conservative 'landed peasantry'. Although problems remained in agriculture, farm owners would not contemplate government interference in their work practices or in the allocation of land.

In such a setting, it is hardly surprising that the Labour Party faced an uphill battle. By the early 1920s it had become a typically European democratic socialist party – containing an equally typical crypto-Marxist left wing. It was also associated with a spirited and active trade union movement. But despite that, Labour's parliamentary representation was dominated for many years by deputies who were principally small town celebrities who had built up strong personal followings. So most of them depended for their return to the Dáil on the votes of essentially right-wing, parochially minded electors. In the cities, where it might have expected to do well, the Labour Party was almost completely outflanked by Fianna Fáil for many years. Fianna Fáil's superior grass-roots organisation and its popular socio-economic policies brought it the support of the majority of the urban working class, and left Labour on the margins.

## Other social cleavages

Cultural–linguistic difference, a social cleavage which is represented in several party systems in Europe, was of relatively slight consequence in the Irish Free State. The main cultural cleavage, between the Protestant unionists and the Catholic nationalists, had been largely removed by the division of the country into two separate states. Further, within the Free State English was almost universally spoken; and the Irish speaking communities of the Gaeltacht never constituted a group with a distinct or separate political identity.

Religion, another important cause of division elsewhere in Europe, was also of little relevance. Partition left the Free State remarkably homogeneous in terms of religion, with around 90 per cent of its population Catholic. Additionally, despite earlier differences with the proponents of independence, the Catholic Church soon identified itself very closely with the new state. This removed the possibility of church-state conflict, and with it the chance of a political party campaigning for secularisation. Although there is an important element of Catholic dissent in Irish political culture, anti-clericalism of the kind found in some other European countries has been of little consequence.

Farming has been a force for political division in many countries, and farmers' parties did emerge in Ireland in the 1920s and 1940s. One of these, appropriately named the Farmers' Party, and formed by the Irish Farmers' Union, was for a time a relatively successful minor party. But though their support was crucial for some governments, they never made an electoral breakthrough – no more than other minor parties which have appealed to just one small section of the electorate. In Ireland, successful 'minor party' TDs have often ended up joining one of the two major groups. (TD is the abbreviation for Teachta Dála, a Member of the Dáil)

### The foundation of Fine Gael

In 1933 the National Centre Party, Cumann na nGaedheal, and the National Guard merged to form Fine Gael. The National Guard, commonly known as the 'Blueshirts', had been formed as an unofficial defence force for Cumann na nGaedheal – which felt threatened by the growing popular support for Fianna Fáil and its relatively recent connections with the anti-Treaty forces in the Civil War. The Blueshirt leader, General Eoin O'Duffy, a former Garda Commissioner (or Chief of Police), actually became the president of Fine Gael. But O'Duffy's fascist predilections became an embarrassment to the party and he was replaced by William Cosgrave, the former leader of Cumann na nGaedheal. Fine Gael is sometimes still taunted by its opponents with the Blueshirt tag, but the party is now as ideologically catch-all as Fianna Fáil. Both main parties refuse to define themselves conclusively as being to the left or the right.

## Coalition politics

The development of Fianna Fáil itself into a catch-all party made the formation of an alternative government exceedingly difficult, and it was not until 1948 that an anti-Fianna Fáil coalition became practicable. The so-called 'inter-party' governments of 1948-51 and 1954-57 involved parties whose policies, particularly on socio-economic issues, were remarkably diverse; but dissimilar parties were inevitably driven together by the dominance of Fianna Fáil. And the main reason for the challenge to Fianna Fáil's predominance in the 1950s was the fact that the economy began to experience severe difficulties. Politicians from all parties had been arguing for a change in economic strategy, but it was Fianna Fáil that finally decided to open the Irish economy to foreign trade, when it returned to office in 1957. Tariffs and quotas on imports would be removed, and incentives would be provided to foreign firms to set up in Ireland.

The change in economic policy did induce economic growth. This led to reductions in both unemployment and emigration, and a real increase in living standards. The new economic prosperity gained Fianna Fáil considerable electoral support, enabled it to win four consecutive general elections, and kept it in office for another sixteen-year period. During this second era of extended Fianna Fáil rule, there were several developments in the party system. Firstly, the 1960s saw a decrease in the number of parties. In 1961 seven different parties sat in the Dáil along with six independents; by 1969 only the three major parties had seats, along with one independent. Secondly, the two opposition groups, Labour and Fine Gael, had become disillusioned with the coalition strategy. Both had found the previous coalitions unsatisfactory, particularly that of 1954-57. Moreover, each of them also believed that they were on the verge of an electoral breakthrough in the early 1960s. However, the failure of either Fine Gael or Labour to make any significant headway in 1969 brought the question of coalition back on to the agenda – Fine Gael won only slight improvements in its votes and seats, while Labour actually lost ground. Both parties realised that without the other's cooperation neither could expect to be in office for the foreseeable future. As a result, they agreed a coalition strategy for the 1973 general election.

---

**The single transferable vote**

Fighting an election as a coalition can be of great value, because of the Irish electoral system. This is proportional representation (PR) by the single transferable vote (STV), in multi-member constituencies. Each constituency returns between three and five TDs. The elector can vote for all the candidates, listing them in order of preference. A quota is worked out by the following formula:

$$\frac{Total\ valid\ poll}{Number\ of\ seats + 1} + 1$$

When a candidate reaches the quota, he or she is elected. The surplus of the candidate's votes above the quota is then allocated to the other candidates, according to the preferences recorded on the ballot paper. Thus, if two parties have a coalition pact before an election, they can ask their supporters to give their second preference vote to the partner party.

---

The benefits of a pre-election pact were clear after the 1973 general election. Although Fianna Fáil increased its vote slightly, it lost six seats. Fine Gael also increased its vote slightly but gained four seats, while Labour dropped by 3 per cent in the poll. Nevertheless, the coalition won five more seats than their combined total in 1969, due almost entirely to the transfer of votes between them.

In the run-up to the general election in 1977, however, the coalition partners failed to note some ominous signs. After the 1973 defeat, Fianna Fáil had overhauled its organisation and had set out to capture the 'youth vote'. This section of the population was, and remains, extremely important, because around 50 per cent of Irish people – and thus a significant part of the electorate – are under twenty-five. Fianna Fáil appealed to the voters with a combination of tax reductions and new jobs. It won eighty-four seats, an increase of sixteen over its 1973 total, while Fine Gael lost eleven and Labour three. For only the second time in the history of the state a party had won over 50 per cent of the vote.

## The economy strikes back

Given the impressive position of Fianna Fáil in 1977, it might have been expected to be embarking on another long spell in office. This was not to be the case. The major reason for the decline in the party's popularity was its inability to deliver on its promises. With increased tension in Northern Ireland, Charles Haughey, who had become party leader and Taoiseach in 1979, singled out the unification of Ireland as the most important issue in the election of 1981. Fine Gael, by contrast, concentrated on the economy, and won more seats and votes than ever before. In the new Dáil, Fine Gael had sixty-five seats, Fianna Fáil seventy-eight and Labour fifteen. The coalition partners, with more seats between them than Fianna Fáil, agreed on a joint programme and formed a government. This coalition, which depended on the tacit support of some independents, lasted until February 1982.

The February 1982 election changed the government again, but only briefly. Fianna Fáil gained three seats, making a total of eighty-one, and formed a government with the support of an independent and the small Workers' Party. The new administration was only able to stay in office until November 1982, however, because after swingeing cuts in social services, the Workers' Party withdrew its support and the government fell. In the general election that followed Fianna Fáil lost six seats, Fine Gael gained seven and Labour one. This gave Fine Gael and Labour a combined overall majority, and another coalition government was formed.

### The 'new right'

The failure of Fianna Fáil to regain its traditional position as the 'natural' governing party of the Republic precipitated a challenge to the leadership of Charles Haughey. Opposition to the party leader was based on his style of leadership, his stance on Northern Ireland, and his conservative views on moral issues such as divorce. There were also reservations about his attitude to the economy. He favoured increased spending to promote growth and job creation, while others in the party wanted more controls on expenditure. A challenge to Haughey by his main rival, Desmond O'Malley, failed, and O'Malley and several other TDs eventually left Fianna Fáil to form the Progressive Democrats (PDs). The PDs are clearly on the political 'right', in the classic mould of European liberals but, in Irish terms, are radical on some important social issues. The emergence of such a party may be a sign of further developments to come in the party system.

### The demands of austerity

The main theme dominating the Dáil after 1982 was, once more, the state of the economy. The coalition had attempted to reduce Ireland's foreign borrowing, without success; and although it managed to cut the inflation rate dramatically, unemployment soared, and with it emigration. In January 1987 Fine Gael introduced a budget involving widespread cutbacks in government expenditure. The Labour deputies were unable to support the welfare reductions involved so they resigned and provoked an election.

Fine Gael fought the general election on its austerity budget. The PDs adopted the economic strategy of the 'new right', including decreasing substantially government involvement in the economy, privatisation, reduced spending on welfare provision and large tax cuts. Fianna Fáil accepted that 90 per cent of the Fine Gael budget would have to be introduced, but it committed itself to investing in targeted areas to increase economic growth, to create jobs and maintain welfare benefits. Labour said that welfare benefits would have to be maintained and the tax net widened to increase the contribution made by farmers and the self-employed.

The outcome of the 1987 election was a minority Fianna Fáil government. An examination of the results, however, revealed some cause for concern for Ireland's dominant party. While Fianna Fáil voters transferred their preferences overwhelmingly to candidates within the party, these candidates received relatively few transfers from outside. Further, the PDs made some significant inroads on Fianna Fáil territory, especially where former Fianna Fáil members stood in the PD interest. Perhaps most significant for the future of the Irish party system was a trend for Fianna Fáil to lose support among the middle classes. Overall Fianna Fáil received its lowest share of the vote in twenty-six years, Fine Gael its lowest for thirty years, and Labour made its worst showing in fifty-four years. In contrast, the PDs made the most dramatic debut for a new party in forty years.

The task of the minority government was eased considerably by the decision of Fine Gael to offer conditional support for its central policies. The main parties were all agreed on the need for sharp reductions in public spending and reduced government borrowing. Though it was defeated five times in the Dáil, the government lost no crucial vote. Nevertheless, the Taoiseach, Haughey, was tempted into calling a election in June 1989 – mainly, it would seem, because opinion polls were indicating that the government might win an overall majority. In the event, Fianna Fáil lost seats, despite securing 44 per cent of first preference votes – the same as in 1987. Its performance only served to emphasise Fianna Fáil's new dependence on other parties.

Fine Gael and the Progressive Democrats had themselves entered into an agreement on coalition during the election campaign. The PDs lost heavily, however, and although Fine Gael did improve by four seats, the parties' combined total of sixty-one was well short of the eighty-four needed for a Dáil majority. The left-wing parties, Labour and the Workers' Party, had fared better, but ruled out any participation in government. Ireland was thus faced with several weeks of uncertainty, before an apparently unlikely coalition government involving Fianna Fáil and the Progressive Democrats was formed in mid-July.

### Whither Fianna Fáil?

The major question for Irish politics posed by the 1989 general election is again about the future role of Fianna Fáil. Since its foundation in 1926 the party has provided single-party government on fourteen out of nineteen possible occasions. Fianna Fáil traditionally eschewed coalitions, representing itself as *the* national party; but it has failed to maintain its early hegemony. Indeed, it looks likely for the future that Fianna Fáil will only be able to rule by sharing power.

The party's dominance of Irish politics received a further blow in November 1990 when the left-wing independent, Mary Robinson, won the presidential election. A one-time member of Seanad Eireann, and closely associated with several liberal causes, she had a comfortable victory, after the second count, over Fianna Fáil's Brian Lenihan and Fine Gael's Austin Currie. Mrs Robinson was proposed as a candidate by the Labour Party, of which she had formerly been a member, and had the support of the Workers' Party and other left-wing groupings. The Progressive Democrats did not formally recommend any candidate, but several prominent members spoke glowingly of Robinson. During her campaign she rejected the description 'socialist', though her past support for socialism was referred to frequently by her opponents. Nonetheless, for the left in Irish politics, Robinson's poll was taken as a sign that an attractively and sensitively presented campaign can bring electoral success.

In Fine Gael, the reverberations of their defeat were felt almost immediately. Alan Dukes, facing the prospect of a vote of no confidence from the Fine Gael parliamentary party, resigned as leader and was replaced by John Bruton. Though Fianna Fáil's vote in the presidential election was the same as in the previous general election, the 1990 result represented a major disappointment. Furthermore, the presidential election was the sixth occasion under Charles Haughey at which it had failed to win a national contest. Many party supporters were questioning the leadership's approach to coalition with the Progressive Democrats, to party organisation and to the presidential campaign.

Disappointment at the presidential election was followed for Fianna Fáil by major reverses at the local government contests in June 1991. Haughey's position as leader was undermined by tension between himself and O'Malley, PD leader and coalition partner, and by unrest within Fianna Fáil itself. Having survived several direct and indirect challenges to his position, Haughey resigned from office in January 1992 when the PDs threatened to leave the coalition. Albert Reynolds succeeded Haughey as leader, and the partnership with the PDs survived until November. Despite all the portents, however, many in Fianna Fáil still thought a single party government was achievable. If the party broadened its appeal by adopting aspects of what has come to be known as 'the liberal agenda', while highlighting the instability of coalition arrangements, Fianna Fáil could, it was felt, still secure a Dáil majority.

The immediate cause of the November 1992 general election was a clash over evidence given by the PD and Fianna Fáil leaders to a public inquiry into possible malpractice in the beef industry. The parties had also differed sharply over the administration of industrial development policy, and about the wording of a referendum question on abortion. Nevertheless, it was the beef tribunal and Reynolds' responsibility for actually calling the election that dominated the campaign. Their leader's unconvincing explanations of his position on both issues weakened Fianna Fáil.

The result (see Table 2.1) was the worst vote for the party since 1927, the year it entered the Dáil for the first time. By contrast,

Table 2.1 *The 1992 general election*[a]

| Party | 1st preference votes | | | Seats | | | |
| | No. | % | Change | No. | % | Change | Candidates |
|---|---|---|---|---|---|---|---|
| Fianna Fáil | 674,650 | 39.1 | −5.1 | 68 | 40.9 | −9 | 122 |
| Fine Gael | 422,106 | 24.5 | −4.8 | 45 | 27.1 | −10 | 91 |
| Labour Party | 333,013 | 19.3 | +9.8 | 33 | 19.9 | +18 | 42 |
| PDs | 80,787 | 4.7 | −0.8 | 10 | 6.0 | +4 | 20 |
| Democratic Left | 47,945 | 2.8 | — | 4 | 2.4 | — | 20 |
| Sinn Féin | 27,809 | 1.6 | +0.4 | — | — | | 41 |
| Green Party | 24,110 | 1.4 | −0.1 | 1 | 0.6 | — | 19 |
| Workers' Party | 11,533 | 0.7 | [b] | — | — | [b] | 18 |
| Others | 102,900 | 6.0 | +2.1 | 5 | 3.0 | — | 109 |
| *Total* | 1,724,853 | 100 | — | 166 | 100 | — | 482 |

*Notes:*

Electorate:2,557,036. Total votes: 1,751,351. Turnout: 68.5 per cent.

Valid vote: 1,724,853. Invalid votes: 26,498. Invalid: 1.5 per cent.

[a] For further comparative election figures, see Chapter 6.

[b] Comparisons based on the Workers' Party performance in 1989 are not given due to the subsequent split in the party.

*Source: Irish Political Studies, Vol. 8, 1993, p.116.*

Labour's representation increased from fifteen to thirty-three seats. And although Fine Gael had been reduced from fifty-five to forty-five deputies, a return to a Fine Gael-led coalition seemed highly probable. The PDs had secured an additional four seats through an electoral strategy of concentrating on a few con-stituencies, and the party seemed destined to be part of a 'rainbow coalition'. Following a lengthy period of discussion, however, a Fianna Fáil/Labour government was formed, based on an agreed programme, in January 1993.

## A major watershed

For Fianna Fáil, 1992 signalled a major watershed. The party faced a future as the leader in the electoral market, but not suffi-ciently dominant to achieve office on its own. Its rural base remained strong, but the party recognised the need to halt the erosion of its working-class support in Dublin. The choice of Dubliner Bertie Ahern as party leader in 1994, and a change in the way it appeals for voting transfers at by-elections, signalled a new realism in Fianna Fáil. Fine Gael also faced serious problems: despite remaining the Republic's second largest party, its candidate finished third in the presidential election of 1990; although Fine Gael achieved 39 per cent of the popular vote at the start of the 1980s, the party has failed to exceed 30 per cent in all general elections since then; and the formation of a Fianna Fáil/Labour coalition with the largest parliamentary majority ever seemed to confine Fine Gael to an unpromising opposition role for the foreseeable future.

The Fianna Fáil/Labour government's programme was based on common centre-left aspirations, and on similar approaches to Northern Ireland policy. The new government enjoyed early economic success, with high growth and low inflation. It also concluded a broad agreement with the UK government in December 1993, the so-called Downing Street Declaration, which was followed in August 1994 by an IRA ceasefire. Despite this good fortune, trust between the two party leaders, Albert Reynolds and Dick Spring, broke down and the government fell. The precipitating events were the publication of the Beef Tribunal Report in July, and disagreement over a judicial appointment in November 1994. An election was not necessary, however, since Fine Gael, Labour and the small left-wing party, Democratic Left (DL), were able to agree on the formation of a new coalition government led by John Bruton, which took office in December 1994.

Democratic Left's inclusion in the 1994 government with Fine Gael shows the remarkable fluidity of parliamentary politics in the Republic. DL developed, through an number of splits and name changes, from the Sinn Féin of the late 1960s. The definitive voice of militant republicanism, Sinn Féin, questioned the legitimacy of constitutional politics, and supported the armed campaign of the IRA for Irish unity. In the early 1970s, however, a number of socialist-minded members split from Sinn Féin, and eventually emerged as a separate group styling itself 'Sinn Féin – the Workers' Party', later simply: the Workers' Party.

Although it began from a fairly orthodox Marxist–Leninist position, and cultivated links with the Soviet Union and its allies, the Workers' Party eventually moved into the democratic social-ist mainstream, and preached working-class unity as the cure for Northern Ireland's ills. By 1992, accusations that the party still had links with the Official IRA were shown to have some sub-stance. (The Official IRA had broken away from what became known as the Provisional IRA at the same time as its political counterpart had split from Sinn Féin.) After some internal upheaval, and in an effort to close the chapter of association with violence once and for all, a substantial part of the party left to form a new grouping. Six of the Workers' Party deputies and a majority of its membership formed Democratic Left, led by the former Workers' Party leader Prionsias De Rossa. Democratic Left remains a radical party with largely working-class electoral support; but it has clearly moved a long way in joining Fine Gael in government.

### Left–right politics at last?

Many observers now speculate that Ireland will develop a class-based party system similar to that in other European countries in the fairly near future. If so, the Progressive Democrats, who made such a spectacular showing at their first general election, might just emerge as the party of the middle class. The PDs' per-formances in 1989 and 1992, however, show that they must compete with Fine Gael for that section of the electorate. Indeed, it is possible that some future understanding on voting transfers and post-election agreements may see these two parties arrive at a long term pact. Yet in the face of the 1994 three-party coalition, cooperation with Fianna Fáil is a more likely short term tactic.

The 1989 and 1992 elections again showed that Fianna Fáil is also increasingly a party of the middle class; and, though it remains the strongest single party among all classes, its tradi-tional working-class support is being eroded by both Labour and

Democratic Left. The Labour Party's claim to be the major left-wing force in the Republic was enhanced by its much increased vote both in 1989 and 1992. It also gained considerably from the successful campaign of Mary Robinson, in which it took a leading role.

Labour's long term strategy, however, has been to increase its distinctive left-wing appeal, but this is hard to do following coalitions with both Fine Gael and Fianna Fáil. Many Labour deputies fear losing votes in working-class and urban areas to their present coalition colleagues in Democratic Left; opinion polls and by-election results lend some weight to their view. Indeed, it was because Democratic Left had won two significant by-elections since 1992 that its votes were sufficient to give the three parties a Dáil majority. Nevertheless, polls also show that Labour's impressive 19 per cent vote in 1992 was due to middle-class voters crossing from Fianna Fáil and Fine Gael, rather than changes in working-class voting.

For the moment, then, Ireland looks like retaining its distinctive party system, with two large catch-all parties and a varying number of smaller groupings. The Progressive Democrats have established themselves as a permanent force, unlike the many other small parties that came and went very quickly. Democratic Left also seems assured of its place, having successfully repositioned itself in the electoral market following the split with the Workers' Party.

In the long run, however, it is difficult in such a small and socially homogeneous country to oust the established parties. The conservative economic outlook of the landowning Irish farm family, the relative smallness of the urban proletariat, the importance of the symbols of national unity, the broad consensus on social values, and the corporatist approach to economic policy militate against radical changes in the party system.

## The style of political competition

The stability of the party system, the lack of deep ideological divisions between the main parties, and a tradition of strict party discipline in the Oireachtas have had an important effect on the way individual politicians compete for election. Irish electors generally remain faithful to one political party. Elections are won or lost by relatively few voters switching their support, and by the success of parties in persuading their traditional supporters to cast their votes. When new parties do emerge, their success is often shortlived.

## The effect of STV PR

Under STV in multi-member constituencies, individual politicians must compete not only against the candidates of other parties, but also against fellow party nominees. Fianna Fáil or Fine Gael may win or lose, but the main priority for each politician is that he or she is personally successful. To ensure success regardless of party fortunes, a politician must have some basis of support among the electorate other than partisan allegiance. Politicians of earlier generations could often rely on being supported because of their role in the struggle for independence or their stand during the Civil War. Today no candidate can be so assured. Clearly the parties do not allow open displays of disagreement at election time, so candidates of the same party cannot compete for support based on policy. Irish politicians, therefore, emphasise their social, local and personal links with the electorate.

Personal support is generally based on the exchange of favours, or the illusion of a favour. Most Irish people continue to believe that public authorities are best approached by some intermediary or influential person. The basis for this belief may lie in the centuries of domination by a colonial power, but it has persisted long after independence. Thus, people are not identified primarily in their formal roles as lawyers, business people, councillors, ministers, etc., but in the first place as friends, or friends of friends, or relatives of friends or people with whom there is some close contact or reciprocal basis for a favour. The use of such contacts and the calling-in of favours is considered legitimate by those with the authority and influence, as well as by those seeking to use the same. The need for local intermediaries is reinforced by the relatively low level of subjective civic competence. This has had the effect of producing politicians who are primarily brokers rather than legislators. Much of an Irish politician's time is taken up telephoning or writing to government ministers, civil servants, local government managers and others in authority on behalf of constituents.

In multi-member constituencies, politicians try to gather sufficient personal support to be elected ahead of their party colleagues. Each candidate will ask for a first preference vote for him or herself, and subsequent votes for fellow party nominees. But the greatest rivalries in Irish politics are often within parties, rather than between them. A substantial personal following insulates the sitting TD from the effects of his party's occasional unpopularity. For some deputies, such as the leading PDs, it may help their election after a change of party. Irish and foreign commentators frequently forecast the end of this 'brokerage' system in the face of increased education, wealth and sophistication. Nevertheless, the system remains important. The importance of social and local connections to politicians' careers is examined further in Chapter 3.

## Other voting opportunities

Elections are not the only occasions on which voters express their opinions. Richard Sinnott has analysed the results of the three referendums of 1992 (see Table 5.2, p. 103), and suggests that:

> On secular-confessional issues, the Republic of Ireland is a deeply divided society . . . [The referendums] point to the existence of three groups of voters each constituting . . . close to 30 per cent of the active electorate.[1]

Sinnott calls the groups: 'ultra-conservatives', who voted 'no' to all three referendum questions; 'liberals', who said 'yes' to the rights to travel and information, but 'no' on the substantive issue of abortion; and 'pragmatists', who gave support to the 'yes' side of each question. This threefold division of the electorate shows that attitudes to moral and religious issues are quite complex. Any party aligning itself with the extremes would risk alienating a significant middle ground. This would be a poor strategy for a large party, but might represent a worthwhile course for a group aiming at a niche in the electoral market. At present, however, the use of referendums to settle major issues of morality means that the parties can avoid too damaging an alignment with the extremes.

### Conclusion

The party system in Ireland is different from most European party systems, because it is not based as much as elsewhere on social cleavages. This is principally because such cleavages were relatively weak at the formation of the system. The major issue after independence in 1922 was the Anglo-Irish Treaty. The division it produced formed the basis of the Irish party setup as we know it today. This issue has, however, subsided since the 1930s. The success of Irish parties now depends on their economic appeal to the electorate, and on the loyalty of their traditional supporters.

Alternative solutions to economic problems have long been the mainstay of Irish general election campaigns. Fianna Fáil's predominance in the electoral system owes much to its record of advancing the economic prosperity of the country. It did this from 1932 to 1948 with its policy of economic self-sufficiency. When this strategy reached the limits of its usefulness, the electorate began to look to other parties, and to vote against the incumbent government. In the four consecutive general elections of 1948, 1951, 1954 and 1957, governments were voted *out* of office.

The Fianna Fáil government of 1957 developed a new economic strategy, based on industrialisation by foreign investment. The economic prosperity that resulted enabled it to win a further three general elections: the election of 1973 ended Fianna Fáil's second run of sixteen years in office. It also ushered in a new period of uncertainty in Irish politics.

From the beginning of the 1970s until the early 1990s Ireland was faced with growing inflation, unemployment and national debt. Again the electorate tended to vote *against* governments. In the seven general elections from 1969 to 1987, the government has lost office each time. In 1989, though it retained its share of the vote, a Fianna Fáil government was forced into a coalition for the first time, having been denied a clear majority. Today coalition governments are the norm. In 1994 a new government was formed for the first time without the need for a general election. Every party in the Dáil is now a potential government partner. The major question about the Irish party system that is still to be answered, however, is whether the division created by the Sinn Féin split over the 1922 Treaty will give way to one reflecting more explicit class or economic divisions in Irish society.

## Note

1 *The Sunday Tribune*, 1 October 1995

## Further reading

M. Busteed, *Voting Behaviour in the Republic of Ireland: a Geographic Perspective*, Oxford: Clarendon Press, 1990.

J. Coakley and M. Gallagher (eds), *Politics in the Republic of Ireland* (2nd edition), Dublin: Folens, 1993.

M. Gallagher and M. Laver (eds), *How Ireland Voted 1992*, Limerick: PSAI Press, 1993.

R. Sinnott, *Irish Voters Decide: Voting Behaviour in Elections and Referendums since 1918*, Manchester: Manchester University Press, 1995.

# 3

# Elites and pressure groups

Power in Ireland is exercised by a range of private and public institutions, such as large companies, banks, government departments, state-sponsored enterprises and major pressure groups. Private wealth is concentrated in relatively few hands, and control of public resources is also dominated by a small number of individuals. Such a distribution of power is typical in liberal-democratic capitalist societies. In this chapter we will examine the nature of the elites as well as the influence of the main pressure groups. Following Parry, we will take elites to be 'small minorities who appear to play an exceptionally influential part in political and social affairs'.[1]

Studies of countries much larger than Ireland have shown remarkable levels of concentration of power. Some social theorists – notably Weber and Durkheim – have sought to show that as societies develop, individual functions within them become more specialised. To such theorists, the cohesion of the social structure demands coordinating elites. Ironically, as more avenues for individual advancement are opened and people are freed from social traditions, so more specialised power roles are created. Some level of elite coordination appears essential for social stability, therefore, even in democracies.

In Ireland, the number of people in key positions of private and institutional power is small enough for elite members to be known and accessible to each other. Members of the Irish elites may have ascended from different professional paths, but there are often common elements in their educational and social backgrounds. Similarly, some points of convergence can be shown in political and social attitudes. In general terms, the various elites accept the economic values of capitalist development, based on profit-making, and they reject other forms of development. The possession of private property is recognised as justified and necessary, and a degree of active social inequality is seen as functional. The political and administrative elites' outlook on development through the encouragement and defence of manufacturing, trading and agricultural business enterprise, coincides with that of the economic elite.

In this chapter we will examine elites by looking at people who, by occupying positions of influence and control in major institutions, can be described as 'powerful'. It is assumed that once in such elite positions their power is felt by society whether they act consciously to influence particular decisions or not.

## The economic elite

The economic elite is taken to be individuals who own substantial amounts of productive property or who occupy top positions in the most important firms. In Ireland, it has been estimated that 1 per cent of the population owns around one-third of wealth, and 5 per cent account for nearly two-thirds of it. Some reports put the number who are 'poor' at nearly one-third. These figures have been challenged on points of detail, but the general pattern of inequality is plain. At the same time, personal wealth in itself is not a measure of power unless it is associated with institutional or other public status – some wealthy people may make no direct impact on society at large. It is not clear whether Ireland's wealthiest citizens are also part of the managerial elite that now dominates large corporations, banks and other financial institutions. What is clear, however, is that access to political or administrative elite positions is not notably easier for the wealthy. As will be shown below, Irish civil servants and members of the Oireachtas are not marked out by the same social distance from the population they serve as in countries such as Britain.

Many of Ireland's wealthiest citizens retain their wealth as agricultural property. On the whole, however, the pattern of landholding is relatively static. Only 2,319 of Ireland's 263,558 agricultural holdings are above 300 acres. The great majority of farms are owned and operated by the same family from generation to generation. The land reforms of the late nineteenth century reduced considerably the number and influence of large landowners. By contrast, the chief executives of the biggest agricultural cooperatives and other related businesses have become highly influential members of the economic elite. Although many of the largest firms are foreign owned, Irish business executives have also been given increased prominence in recent years, and some, such as the supermarket chain owner, Feargal Quinn, have been active in the public domain.

In manufacturing industry, one-third of the workforce is employed by foreign-owned companies and the running of many Irish factories is actually dependent upon management decisions made abroad. Such foreign firms are most dominant in the larger and expanding industrial projects, so that their economic influence is even greater. The proportion of senior managerial staff in the Irish operations of such foreign enterprises is small; and the major managerial, professional and research functions are unlikely to be carried out in Ireland.

Irish influence in manufacturing mainly comes via the state which, by facilitating both foreign and domestic investment as well as investing directly, is at the centre of industrial activity in its own right. The state bureaucracy at the higher levels sees itself as in the same 'enterprise' as private managers, and in partnership with state sponsored companies. Thus the answer to the question 'Who makes up the economic elite?' – who, in other words, occupies key institutional positions of power – revolves around the identity of senior bureaucrats as well as of managers.

Research on the economic elite in Ireland is very sparse, and many everyday assertions about it are little more than speculation. It is apparent, however, that the economic elite is relatively stable and exercises some 'control' over its own membership. Obviously, the privately wealthy may retain their advantage through the working of inheritance, good accountants, and a relatively favourable tax regime for wealth – as distinct from income. Those of managerial and higher professional status are also restricted by social opportunities as well as by ability. The intra-generational stability of social groupings in Ireland is remarkable. In a study of Dublin, Whelan and Whelan examined the composition of what they call 'the elite classes':

> Thirty-five per cent of the men currently in this higher class are themselves sons of higher professional and managerial fathers; a further 40 per cent are drawn from the other white collar classes and the petty bourgeoisie. Thus, 75 per cent of the occupants of higher professional and managerial classes are drawn from just four classes; the corresponding figure for England and Wales is 47 per cent. Similarly, only 14 per cent of higher professional and managerial respondents had working-class origins, a figure which is half the corresponding one for England and Wales.[2]

Put another way, the chances of a man born into the highest social bracket staying in that group are 240 times greater than those of someone born in the lower classes. These figures are, of course, too global to apply directly to the elites looked at here. Nevertheless, the background to our study of elites is one of high social stability.

Further, in Ireland, a person's first occupation, which is heavily influenced by early educational attainment, has an extremely significant effect upon where in the economic hierarchy he or she is currently employed. In effect, not many people who start in manual and semi-skilled jobs gain professional or managerial posts later in life. One reason for this social rigidity is that participation rates in higher education are many times greater for the offspring of professionals and managers than for other social categories. In addition, some children of the economic elite attend fee-paying secondary schools that offer both educational and social advantages.

During the first thirty years of this century, the upper or 'ascendancy' class associated with the British regime became socially marginalised. The social elite of the new state was decidedly bourgeois, dominated by the mercantile and shopkeeping classes. Historically the Irish bourgeoisie was based essentially on trade. Throughout the eighteenth century, Catholics were prevented from owning land, except on relatively short leases, and were also excluded from public office. They thus directed their energies and wealth into trade – a large proportion of economic activity, especially for an island. Much of the profit earned from this business was invested abroad, and in commercial rather than manufacturing ventures. A main argument for relaxing the 'penal laws', as the anti-Catholic legislation was known, was to encourage the wealth held by Catholics to be invested in the country to increase economic activity. The laws were abolished towards the end of the eighteenth century, but the Catholic bourgeoisie did not put the bulk of their money into industrial development, as was hoped. They had little experience in industrial matters; and there was greater uncertainty in industrial projects in Ireland because of British competition.

At independence, the more prosperous Irish were in trade, farming or the professions. Where they were involved in industry, it tended to be on a small scale. Social mobility for the smaller farmers and tradespeople often involved entry to the traditional professions, which were highly regarded, both for status and security. For these groups, it was the large bureaucracies like the civil service, local government and public administration that provided, and to a large extent still provide, the main channel for upward mobility into the professional and managerial class.

### Political elites

The personalised nature of Irish electoral competition encourages a wide interest in the details of politician's activities. Consequently, directories of national and local politicians are more widely read in Ireland than elsewhere. The most obvious characteristic of deputies, senators and local councillors is that the proportion of men is much higher than in the electorate; in 1996 only 23 of 166 Dáil deputies (13.8 per cent) were women. In this respect Ireland does better than countries such as Britain,

Table 3.1 *Socio-economic background of TDs, 1996*

| Categories | TDs: % | Population as a whole: % |
|---|---|---|
| Higher professional | 24 | 4 |
| Lower professional | 28 | 6 |
| Employers/managers | 17 | 7 |
| Semi-skilled and non-skilled manual | — | 13 |

*Source:* Provisional Report of the Constitutional Review Group, 1996.

the US and Japan, but it still falls below the EU average of just over 18 per cent.

Other characteristics of politicians in Western democracies are also displayed in Ireland (see Table 3.1): deputies are disproportionately drawn from the liberal professions, especially teaching and law; they are also twice as likely to have completed a secondary education, and over three times as likely to have a university degree as the general population. Though farmers are much in evidence in the Dáil, they are under-represented in terms of their numbers in the country as a whole. The dominance of the professional classes is even more marked at ministerial level: almost 60 per cent of ministers since 1922 have come from this group. Business people are also well represented among ministers, although it is sometimes hard to know with what size of enterprises they have links.

The professional background and educational attainment of politicians do not tell us anything about their views or policy preferences. To assume, for example, that better-off individuals are less sensitive to the plight of the poor may be misleading. What the evidence does tell us is that certain groups such as manual workers, women and the socially disadvantaged generally do not make it to the top as politicians. Similarly most TDs are in the forty-one to fifty-five age group, though this accounts for only 14 per cent of the population.

As we saw in Chapter 2, it is important for a candidate at an Irish election to become known personally to the electorate. This process is, of course, eased if your 'name' is an already established one. Twenty-three per cent of deputies elected in 1992 were related to former members; indeed, often they are their sons or daughters. 'Heredity', therefore, plays an important part in elite selection. Other forms of ready identification, such as sporting repute, may also help an individual aspiring to the political elite; 15 per cent of incumbents in the 1980s were prominent in sport. The 'parachuting' of well-known names into politics has, however, had little success. This occurs when the central party imposes a candidate on the local organisation because it feels that the available runners do not have a sufficiently high public profile. Indeed, potential candidates such as television personalities, sports stars and pressure group leaders may be approached by more than one party. Generally, however, the imposed candidate gets very little support from local party workers.

The route to the national political elite commonly involves service in local government. Almost 80 per cent of TDs have been councillors. Again, a record of local service helps a would-be deputy establish his or her name in the potential Dáil constituency. Local government experience may be particularly important for a candidate without the social advantages of professional status or educational attainment.

Local government service, local family connections and local prestige are, then, the most important qualifications for entry to the political elite. That elite is not notable for any great social distance from the electorate, though lower status occupations are clearly at a marked disadvantage. Oireachtas membership changes only slowly, despite the competitive rhetoric of elections. Once elected, a deputy or, to a lesser extent, a senator, can expect a reasonably long career. Often, membership of the Seanad is used to introduce new members or to protect electorally defeated members of the political elite, and this adds to the group's stability. Though they are bound to emphasise partisan differences, and subtly establish their own 'personal' images, Irish politicians share many interests and values. Among these are loyalty to parliamentary democracy, to nationalism, to the moral ethos of the Catholic Church, and a belief that politicians collectively make a worthwhile contribution to the nation.

Further, like most stable groups, the political elite is a fairly cohesive informal social network, reflecting common patterns of work, income and leisure.

### Administrative elites

The political elite, as defined above, includes all members of the Oireachtas. This is almost certainly too broad if the criteria for inclusion features a direct and sustained influence on policy. One group, however, represents an established centre of power. After independence, the Free State bureaucracy became as central an institution as its British predecessor. The enormous importance of the civil service and, to a lesser extent, the state sponsored bureaucracies was heightened by the dominance of the public sector in the rather underdeveloped economy of the post-independence period. Because of its political indispensability, the civil service was able to retain its corporate integrity and identity, and to resist pressures towards politicisation. The result of this situation was the creation and survival of a 'powerful bureaucracy', independent of the party machine.

Here we will look primarily at the higher civil servants, those at Principal Officer level and above. In 1994, 457 people were in such positions. These posts are recognised as crucial because their occupants control vital information, and supply advice to senior political office holders. As we will see in Chapter 4, higher civil servants often make important policy decisions independently of politicians, and they certainly shape policy significantly. Of course, senior politicians do have sources of advice outside the civil service, but in Ireland, more than in most democracies, power is highly centralised in the state bureaucracy. The most senior public servants at local government level are the county or city managers; this group is, therefore, briefly examined here also.

The recruitment and promotion procedures of the Irish public service, local and national, are formally and rigorously meritocratic. The central tenet is the merit principle, which means that persons selected for posts in the public service must have the requisite skill and knowledge. Though public service recruitment is controversial elsewhere, particularly in newly independent states, in Ireland there has been no sustained challenge to the system, based as it is on the possession of qualifications. It is assumed such an arrangement removes the dangers of ineffi- ciency and favouritism associated with political appointments. Civil servants and local government officers are recruited by the civil service and Local Appointments Commissions respectively. The political neutrality and absolute independence of these bodies are not in doubt.

Most civil servants (other than those in specialised technical grades) join the public service at junior levels straight from school, though the proportion of graduate entrants is increas- ing. A similar trend towards graduate entry may occur at local government level now that some middle-ranking posts have been opened to graduates. The traditional model for high-level public servants has been junior entry followed by in-service training, third-level education through evening classes and day- release, and a steady progress up the ranks via examinations and competitive interviews. The Departments of Finance and Foreign Affairs are exceptions in that most of their senior people enter the service as graduates.

Higher civil servants have their critics, but few can doubt their qualities of industry and ambition. Indeed most criticisms have centred on the presumed dulling effects of such sustained prac- tical and diligent work in a hierarchical organisation. The civil service is accused of being too unimaginative, insulated from ideas in the outside world, and disproportionately concerned with short term objectives. This narrowness of outlook is rein- forced by the absence in Ireland of any significant movement between private and public employment.

The general pattern of promotion, particularly at higher levels, has been for civil servants to rise within one department. Though in recent years there has been greater mobility between depart- ments in filling top posts, many higher civil servants are set in their thinking as regards their own department's area of specialism. This 'departmental line' is obviously tempered by the current political realities, but it may represent an underlying theme in civil service advice. It is plainly difficult to work in a particular area of policy for most of a career and not develop some firm views. Common ideas do provide a certain internal cohesion to the group. To a lesser degree, a commonality of approach has developed throughout the administrative elite, that rests on a sense of its own indispensability, corporate responsibility and self-interest.

The administrative elite work in a system, the main organisational characteristics of which were inherited from Britain. In Ireland, however, the elite is not marked out by social distance from other public servants. There is no tradition of social exclusivity. The main barrier to entry into the public service is educational achievement, which in Ireland has been eased for almost all classes by free or inexpensive secondary schooling. There is a tendency for higher civil servants to have attended schools run by religious orders, but there is no 'old school tie' tradition.

The number of women at the Principal Officer or Counsellor level and above, though small, is growing, as is the number in the Assistant Principal grade. In 1982, 26 per cent of Assistant Principals were women, which is over six times the number in 1972. By 1993 the proportion of female Assistant Principals had hardly changed, but 6 per cent of Assistant Secretaries were women, compared with 1 per cent in 1987. By contrast, in local government, none of the senior posts has ever been held by a woman.

The administrative elite is not marked out educationally, culturally or socially from other Irish elites. The senior civil servant is particularly powerful, however. He or she operates at the core of the highly centralised, secretive, self-protective, pervasive and unrivalled administrative machine outlined in Chapter 4. None of the other elites can bring the same level of sustained, informed and rigorous attention to any public issue as the administrative elite.

Local government managers are also powerful, but are less shielded from public criticism because they are more publicly accountable for their actions and advice. City and County Managers are also further from the key legislative processes. But despite the fact that they remain to some degree subservient to central government, they do have a substantial degree of autonomy from their own local politicians, and are clearly at the hub of the local administration. Indeed, while the approximate equivalents of local government managers employed by the health boards administer major services on behalf of the community, they are even more clearly subordinate to Dublin. Socially and educationally, however, all these administrators are from similar backgrounds to civil servants, the most important difference being that they tend to have served in several parts of the country.

## Major interest groups

One important common feature of the Irish administrative elite is a high level of self-conscious nationalism. This attitude is a product both of Ireland's comparatively recent independent status, and of its proximity to a much more powerful and older state. In part this nationalism is expressed in the support given to the Irish language, as a symbol of identity and separateness. More importantly, however, it is reflected in elite's positive attitudes to economic development, and relative lack of concern about environmental and social disruption. The elites' outlook as regards such development gives the representatives of economic interest groups an important 'insider' status in the formulation of public policy. It also fashions the terms of public discussion, and gives an advantage to those who can present their private interests as being congruent with the national interest.

The major economic interest groups – employers, trade unions and farming organisations – are portrayed as 'social partners' with government. Their participation in policy formulation is formalised in numerous advisory and consultative bodies such as the National Economic and Social Council (NESC). In October 1987 the social partners arrived at an agreement, the 'Programme for National Recovery' (PNR), which was to dictate the level of pay rises and social benefits for a period of three years. The programme was evidence of the so-called 'corporatist' style of policy-making in Ireland – as were its predecessors, the 'National Agreements' and 'National Under-standings'. The main difference between the PNR and previous arrangements was that it involved the agricultural sector as well as the government, business and the unions. It was followed by a similar agreement in 1991, called the 'Programme for Economic and Social Progress' (PESP), and another in 1994, the 'Programme for Competitiveness and Work' (PCW), both part of a ten-year corporatist strategy. *The Irish Times* mirrored a widely held elite view when it claimed that, 'The social partnership developed between government, employers and workers [has] been an essential building block of economic growth.'[3]

## The employers

The two main groups representing employers' interests, the Confederation of Irish Industry and the Federated Union of Employers, merged in November 1992 to form IBEC: the Irish Business and Employers' Confederation. IBEC represents some four thousand companies and organisations from all sectors of economic and commercial activity. It is funded by subscriptions and fees, provides economic data and analysis for its members, and represents business interests in negotiations with the trade unions and government. Through its Brussels office, the Irish Business Bureau, it also works on behalf of business and employers at EU level. The influence of multinational companies in Ireland has led some commentators to predict a decline in the role of IBEC. As a result, corporatism would also decline as a means of managing the economy. Multinationals are, after all, controlled by global considerations. Despite this argument, most large foreign firms have adopted a 'when in Rome' policy to local business practice and have been fully supportive of IBEC and its lobbying activities.

## The trade unions

Despite the republican socialist/syndicalist leadership of James Connolly, James Larkin and others in the second decade of this century, the trade union movement in Ireland has, by and large, stood aside from involvement in the national question. Connolly's vision went beyond the purely nationalist struggle. He argued that freedom from Britain was only a part of the greater struggle for freedom from the capitalist system. As Connolly put it: 'If you remove the English army tomorrow and hoist the green flag over Dublin Castle, unless you set about the organisation of the Socialist Republic your efforts would be in vain!'[4] Larkin, for his part, saw the unions as the key mechanism in advancing the achievement of a socialist organisation of society. However, following the defeat of the unions in the great 1913 Dublin lockout, Larkin went to America (where he was jailed for a period for subversion) and did not return until after independence; and Connolly was shot for his part in the Easter Rising.

The new leadership of the Irish Trade Union Congress (ITUC) had a more restricted view of the political role of the workers, as regards both the developing independence struggle and the pursuit of socialism. Partition was, of course, a problem for the trade unions, but more for institutional than for political reasons. The ITUC remained intact as the trade union centre for the whole of Ireland, but many of its affiliated unions were British based and continued to organise in the Free State. After independence, therefore, tensions between the new and growing Irish-based unions and the long-established British unions were inevitable. There came to be a particular enmity between the two largest organisations – the Irish Transport & General Workers (ITGWU), and the British-based Amalgamated Transport & General Workers (ATGWU). This culminated in 1944 in the breakaway from the ITUC of ITGWU and seventeen other Irish-based unions to form the Congress of Irish Unions (CIU). Despite constant efforts to heal the breach, the CIU and the ITUC remained apart until 1959, when they finally merged to create the Irish Congress of Trade Unions (ICTU).

The ICTU today has 86 affiliated trade unions, representing around 670,000 workers. Of the members in unions affiliated to the ICTU, roughly 445,000 are in the Republic (in 60 or so unions) and 225,000 in Northern Ireland (just over forty unions); there are 18 unions with members in both the Republic and Northern Ireland. The three largest unions until recently were ITGWU, ATGWU and the Federated Workers' Union of Ireland (FWUI), which together held the great majority of members. Those few unions not affiliated to the ICTU represent around 10 per cent (or 70,000) of unionised workers. Union membership in the Republic, as a proportion of people in work, is relatively stable (over 45 per cent – compared to approximately 30 per cent in Britain). There have recently been some important union mergers, designed mainly to achieve economies of scale and, hopefully, a better service to members. In 1990 the ITGWU and the FWUI joined forces to form the Services, Industrial, Professional, Technical Union (SIPTU), which has well over 200,000 members. Similarly, the bodies representing many local government and civil and service employees are now merged in IMPACT with a membership of around 35,000.

The ICTU has no formal position on partition, except to the extent that it has always insisted that there must be no change in the status of Northern Ireland without the consent of the people there. Associated with that, it has also been among the strongest opponents of the use of violence for political purposes. As for the party politics of the Republic, the ICTU tends towards a non-partisan position, perhaps in the knowledge that Fianna Fáil has always attracted more of the working-class vote than the Labour Party. Despite the continuing reservations of some of its major affiliates, the ICTU has been a steady supporter of the centralised, corporatist agreements such as the PNR, PESP and PCW.

## The farmers

Land has traditionally held an important position for Irish people. Until the 1930s it was seen as the lifeblood of the economy, and it still makes a major contribution to the wealth of the country. But land, and the people who work it, have long been regarded as much more than economic assets. The ownership of land is charged with much social, political and cultural significance. The model of the family farm remains an important part of Ireland's self-image. The transfer of ownership effected in the late nineteenth century means that now more than 90 per cent of Irish farmers own their land.

One of the two largest farming organisations, the Irish Creamery Milk Suppliers' Association (ICMSA) was founded in 1950 to campaign on behalf of farmers who produced milk. The bulk of milk production used to come from small farms, but this pattern has now changed with 12 per cent of suppliers providing 40 per cent of the milk sent to creameries. The number of milk suppliers has reduced in recent years and now stands at about 58,000. The ICMSA has, therefore, had to broaden its appeal. The ICMSA was formerly a very militant organisation, and in 1953 called a successful sixteen-day strike in support of its demand for an increase in the price paid to farmers for their milk. But within a few years, the ICMSA came to be regarded as fairly conservative. It believes in intensification of agricultural production on small farms; and it is suspicious of land reform and of EU programmes for modernisation and the retirement of elderly farmers. The ICMSA has its headquarters in Limerick and organises its 52,000 members through 480 branches throughout the country.

The main farming organisation, however, is the Irish Farmers' Association (IFA). The IFA grew out of the National Farmers' Association (NFA), which was set up in 1955. It developed into a highly efficient body, and employed agricultural experts to present its case to government for improvements in farming and farm incomes. By the mid-1960s the IFA was recognised by government as the farmers' representative to be consulted regularly on the formulation of agricultural policy. The IFA was very militant in the 1960s, reflecting farmers' anger at their economic difficulties. There was the feeling among the farming community that it had been left behind by an economic plan that concentrated on the development of an Irish industrial sector. During the militant campaigns of the 1960s, farmers went to gaol as a result of protests.

Today, the IFA is much more integrated into the national policy-making system. With a membership of over 150,000, it is regarded by many as Ireland's most effective interest group. For example, even before Irish entry to the EU, the IFA had opened an office in Brussels. The IFA also believes in increasing production in farming in response to market conditions, and unlike the ICMSA, it signed the PNR in 1987. The ICMSA's failure to sign arose from an ill-judged attempt to gain last minute concessions on its proposal for a land-tax. By the time of the PESP, the ICMSA's position on tax was no longer an impediment to its signature. The farmer's representatives are now full 'social partners'.

Two further organisations are also an important part of the farm lobby. The Irish Co-operative Organisation articulates the views of a crucial section of the fast-growing food industry. Its voice is of increasing importance because of major restructuring in recent years. Macra na Feirme lobbies on behalf of young farmers on such issues as inheritance taxes and agricultural education. It has over 10,000 members and many powerful figures in agricultural politics are former members.

The greatest overall improvement for Irish agriculture came with entry to the EU. As well as bringing higher and guaranteed prices, the EU has attempted to modernise farming, by encouraging the enlargement of farms, the use of better technology and the education of farmers. Though the number of small farms (under 30 acres) has declined, the rate of decline has been much slower than many expected. The leaders of agricultural opinion have helped shift the rhetoric of policy towards a recognition of the changing source of total farm household income; and there has been much less stress on the frugality, spirituality and cosiness of rural life as envisaged by Eamon de Valera. The political, administrative and agricultural elites agree on the need to ensure the competitiveness of the upper income farmers; on the necessity to retain or achieve viability for the middle income group; and on the importance of addressing the problems of current low earners, through social policy and encouragement of land mobility.

## The Catholic Church

One powerful force in Ireland that has had, and continues to have, a major influence on Irish society is the Catholic Church.

In 1911, almost 90 per cent of the population of the twenty-six counties which were to make up the Irish Free State were Catholics. This figure has increased to over 95 per cent at present. The proportion of committed and practising Catholics in Ireland marks it off from other EU countries with high Catholic populations. Before independence, government in Ireland was a predominantly Protestant business. The Catholic Church supported the nationalist movement, and kept its distance from the government. After independence this aloofness was maintained. In other countries conflict arises between church and state because the church wishes to extend, maintain or defend its influence in the face of increased state activity. In the Free State, there was no major driving force for the secularisation of the new state. Some influential and senior clerics urged Irish governments to enact distinctly Catholic legislation. At the same time, there was no general desire on the church's part to extend its authority, because it was satisfied with the influence it already had.

In respect of social welfare services, for instance, the Church has a stake that might seem extensive to visitors from Protestant countries. The state does not attempt to provide all such services itself, and many hospitals, orphanages, juvenile reformatories and other welfare institutions are run by Catholic religious orders, with the aid of government grants and, to varying extents, under government control. The interpenetration of church and state is seen most clearly in the field of education. Education is not merely denominationally controlled: it is clerically controlled.[5]

In the conclusion of his definitive study, Whyte looks at two opposing propositions on the influence of the Catholic Church in Ireland. On the one hand, he disagrees with the assertion that Ireland is a theocratic state 'in which the hierarchy has the final say on any matter in which it wishes to intervene'. In his view, the total record does not show that Irish governments 'have automatically deferred to the hierarchy on any point on which the hierarchy chooses to speak'.[6] On the other hand, he feels that the notion that the church is only one among a number of interest groups in society to be naïve. For in the final analysis, in a mainly Catholic country, the Catholic hierarchy has a weapon that no other group possesses: its authority over people's consciences. Most politicians are practising Catholics, and accept the hierarchy's right to speak on matters of faith or morals. Even politicians who are personally indifferent to religion recognise that most of the electorate are believers, and will act accordingly.[7]

In the past, the Church's influence had much to do with the social structure in Ireland. This consisted largely of rural communities where priests found it relatively easy to exercise control over the inhabitants. But the situation has changed decisively because of urbanisation and industrialisation. Urban dwellers and the young are more willing to question established social and moral values, while increased disposable income, foreign travel, newspapers and television have led to an erosion of religiosity in Ireland.

The lessening of the church's influence has been reflected in changes in the laws governing such issues as the availability of contraceptives, the censorship of books and films, and the legalisation of homosexual activity. In 1995 a narrow majority voted in a referendum for the introduction of divorce, despite direct appeals from the Pope and the Irish hierarchy. Moreover, much evidence has accumulated on the widening gap between the attitudes to religion between the old and the young, and between those living in Dublin and those outside the capital. By October 1995 many commentators were talking about a 'Church in crisis'. An opinion poll in the Dublin *Sunday Tribune* claimed that 'a staggering 75 per cent of people have mixed or little or no confidence at all in their church leaders'. Again, negative views were especially marked among the young. The reasons for this rapid decline in respect are complex. Some are connected to developments in Catholicism internationally, such as a conservative papacy and a retreat from the ideals of Vatican II. Others are related to a series of revelations of serious sexual misconduct at every level of the clergy and religious orders: priests have been convicted of paedophilia; and a senior bishop was revealed to have a son living in the USA. More broadly, the Catholic Church in Ireland has appeared defensive, secretive and unwelcoming of lay involvement at a time when other aspects of Irish life were becoming much more transparent and participative. As Dr William Walsh put it when speaking to a conference of priests in April 1996:

> there is a perception that we, as bishops and other religious authorities, involved ourselves in a web of secrecy that was designed to protect the abuser rather than the abused ... There has been dismay and distress among Catholics at the state of their Church. There has been real grief at the death of their own illusions.[8]

The influence of the Catholic Church over the morals, and especially the sexual morality, of Irish people may have declined, but the church is still powerful and socially pervasive. Ninety-five per cent of all schools are under Catholic management, as are many social and health facilities. Parish clergy are active in all forms of community, sports and social organisations, especially in rural areas. Nuns are to the forefront in many campaigns for social justice. And the church is involved in many aspects of Irish public life, which in other countries are usually the exclusive province of secular authorities.

Finally, demonstrating that the hierarchy is far from being the only source of pressure on the state to support Catholic values, there has been a remarkable increase in lobbying and pressure group activity led by lay people. Furthermore, organisations such as the Society for the Protection of the Unborn Child (SPUC) and the Pro-Life Amendment Campaign (PLAC) have shown that Catholic opinion in Ireland can still be mobilised into a powerful lobby on moral questions. This been particularly evident at times when governmental majorities have been slender.

### The media

Arguably not quite an elite, still less a pressure group in the normally accepted sense, journalists in Ireland certainly *seek* to have an influence on the politics of the nation. Until the 1930s, there were just two main national daily papers. *The Irish Times*, the voice of Irish Unionism before independence, became, and remains, non-party. Ireland's daily 'paper of record', it claims – with some justice – to produce both the most serious and the most radical journalism in the Republic; it is run by a trust, and has a specific brief to advance the cause of a pluralist and more liberal Ireland. *The Irish Independent* and its evening and Sunday sisters are also at the quality end of the market by international standards; supporters of Cumann na nGaedheal during the early years of independence, they are now less uncritical in their backing of its successor, Fine Gael – and frequently espouse 'new right' thinking, especially on the economy.

The lack of a newspaper supporting Fianna Fáil led de Valera to set up *The Irish Press* soon after his party first came to power in the 1930s. It quickly became the most popular paper in Ireland, and led the market for nearly fifty years. However, in the 1980s *The Irish Press* and its evening and Sunday stablemates not only became less closely identified with Fianna Fáil (despite remaining in the hands of the de Valera family), but also fell on hard times. The group was the subject of several rescue attempts, but finally expired in 1995 – occasioning considerable shock and dismay, even among its rivals.

The morning national press now consists of four main papers: the two remaining traditional dailies; *The Daily Star*, a less sensational version of the British paper of the same name (jointly owned by the British Express and the Irish Independent groups); and the successful non-aligned provincial paper, *The Cork Examiner*, relaunched as *The Examiner* in the hope of picking up at least some of the former *Irish Press* readership. Sunday offers a wider choice, including a colourful tabloid specialising in scandal, a specialist business broadsheet, and a paper first published in 1996 devoted entirely to sport. There is also a lively, and often highly political, weekly provincial press in Ireland, meshing neatly with the concern of so many politicians with parish pump issues. At the same time, there are considerable worries about the penetration into Ireland of British newspapers

– the tabloids in particular – which sometimes cost less than half the price of their Irish counterparts.

Irish newspapers are notable for their restraint in reporting on the personal lives of people in the public eye, especially politicians. But like the free press everywhere, they have frequently been the progenitors of major policy change, especially as a consequence of good investigative journalism. The same has been true of Irish radio and television. Radio Telefís Éireann (RTE) is the state broadcasting organisation; it is responsible for two television and three main radio channels, and has recently been joined by a mushrooming independent radio sector. Despite the fact that RTE (like the BBC in Britain and national public broadcasting stations in the USA) is legally required to be politically non-partisan, it has been a significant force for social and, it follows, political change. There is a perception, at the same time, that RTE has lost its cutting edge. Major stories of Irish political interest (such as that which led to the setting up of the tribunal on possible abuses in the beef industry) have been broken on British television – which is of course available almost everywhere in Ireland. This has given added impetus to the drive to set up a third, independent national television network. Also beginning in 1996 was Teilifís na Gaeilge, an Irish language station.

It is notoriously difficult to measure the influence of the press, radio and television on public opinion, still more to gauge the effect which they have in convincing politicians that change is necessary in this or that area of national life. It is nonetheless impossible to deny that free and independent media are crucial components of a modern democracy. In this respect, Ireland seems well served.

## Conclusion

The structure and distribution of power in Ireland is similar to that in other liberal-democratic states. Although Ireland is, in formal terms, a meritocratic country, upward social mobility is restricted. As in other capitalist countries, the most powerful interest groups in Ireland are those concerned with the economy. Employers' organisations accept the State's management of the economy along free market lines; and employees' organisations offer no strong challenge to the broadly capitalist development of Ireland – the trade unions being essentially concerned with defending workers against low pay, poor working conditions and unemployment. The economic, administrative and political elites share a common attachment to an essentially developmental image of the direction in which Ireland is moving – and they are not as distant from the general population as elites in many other countries. The media too are part of this consensus, but can be among the most influential, if intermittent, forces for change.

There are many interest groups in Ireland not directly concerned with the economy. Several have existed for some time and campaign on cultural issues such as the preservation of the Irish language and traditions and the promotion of uniquely Irish sports. In recent years several campaigning groups have grown up to press their views on specific issues, such as military neutrality and combating poverty. Other 'one-issue' campaigns, such as the remarkable push in 1988 against the introduction of the requirement for a licence to go fishing, bring previously non-political groups into public controversy – but only for a short time. Similarly, environmental groups or those concerned to protect Ireland's architectural heritage are occasionally brought to the fore because of some issue that captures the general public's imagination. The non-economic organisation with the strongest influence in Ireland remains, however, the Roman Catholic Church.

Interest groups press their views on public policy through a variety of methods. Usually the most effective are those groups whose views are heard away from the public gaze – those inside the policy 'community' which is dominated by ministers and civil servants. Street protests may show numerical strength or deep conviction, but they often signal a real lack of influence on the formation of public policy.

## Notes

1 G. Parry, *Political Elites*, London: Allen & Unwin, 1967, p. 13.
2 C. Whelan and B. Whelan, *Social Mobility in the Republic of Ireland: a Comparative Perspective*, Dublin: Economic and Social Research Institute, 1984, p. 3.
3 *The Irish Times*, 17 May 1996.
4 J.P. Berresford-Ellis, *James Connolly: Selected Writings*, Harmondsworth: Penguin, 1981, p. 124.
5 J. H. Whyte, *Church and State in Modern Ireland, 1923-79*, Dublin: Gill & Macmillan, 1971, pp. 16-17.
6 *Ibid.*, p. 369.
7 *Ibid.*, p. 368.
8 Cited in *The Irish Times*, 23 April 1996.

## Further reading

R. Breen, D. Hannan, D. Rottman and C. Whelan, *Understanding Contemporary Ireland*, Dublin: Gill & Macmillan, 1990.
P. Clancy, S. Drudy, K. Lynch and L. O'Dowd (eds), *Irish Society: a Sociological Perspective*, Dublin: Institute of Public Administration, 1995.

**4**

# The policy-making process

Public policies are the products of government. They take many forms. Some follow public announcements made with much fanfare in the context of lively public debate. Others evolve from the practice of government, i.e., what civil servants, police officers, teachers and others in authority actually do. Indeed in many areas of public policy there is a considerable gap between what is formally declared to be policy and what actually happens. This is because the process of making policy is much more complex than is conventionally understood. Those most closely involved – ministers, civil servants and other public officials – may indeed contribute to this misunderstanding. They often suggest that the process consists of the politicians deciding policy, while bureaucrats simply administer or carry out their decisions. In this way, citizens are reassured that only those actors who are democratically accountable to the electorate are responsible for the allocation of scarce public resources. The electorate and the media reinforce this politician-centred model. They focus too much attention on the most obvious characters in the political drama: the Taoiseach and his (it is not yet possible to say 'her') ministers, as well as their leading parliamentary opponents.

In this chapter, policy is taken to be what government does rather than simply what is formally described as policy. It is the cumulative impact of laws, rules, orders, incentives and the use of discretion by those in authority, whether they are elected or not. In Ireland, for reasons of electoral pressure and public expectation, many politicians present themselves as able to alter, in individual cases, what central or local government does. Thus, some citizens believe that public policy is the result of endless interventions by politicians in the operation of government departments, local authorities and other public bodies. The Department of Social Welfare, for example, deals with 40,000 representations and 4,000 parliamentary questions per year about its day-to-day operations. Explanations of public policy-making which concentrate on the brokerage activities of politicians are interesting, but mostly because of what they reveal about elections. They are hardly adequate, however, to explain either the vast majority of decisions in which politicians play no direct part or, more importantly, the major decisions that transcend particular individual interests. In this chapter, the process by which major public decisions, such as hospital closures or infrastructural investments, are made is examined. How the public service is organised to deal with such decisions is central to the process.

### External influences on policy

The Republic has undergone many important changes of policy direction, especially since the late 1950s. A long period of protectionism in economic policy, parity between the Irish pound and sterling and the near-total dependence on the British market has ended. By 1985 more goods were exported to the continental EU states than to Britain. Over the same time foreign manufacturing investment has been encouraged, especially in high-technology industries such as computing. Many policy changes have resulted from their new directions in economic strategy. While the Republic's prosperity has increased in recent decades because of economic policy changes, not all the effects have been positive socially, culturally or environmentally.

So whose ideas fashioned these major national decisions – who sets the policy process in train? One answer, which might be drawn from the discussion in Chapter 1, is 'nobody in Ireland, at any rate'! Certainly, as a small state relying on international trade and multinational companies, decisions made in Chicago,

London, Tokyo and elsewhere can have an immediate impact in Ireland. Even a decision to place new investment or orders in other countries with similar levels of development can have a direct impact on Irish public policy. Often such decisions are taken without reference to Ireland at all, but are made for reasons of global commercial strategy. Nevertheless, patterns of employment, education and social expenditure in the Republic are directly affected. Thus, the decision to move a manufacturing operation to Spain may mean more emigration from Mayo, with resultant changes in school, medical and other provision. No Irish voice needs to be heard, at least until the decision on which of Mayo's schools or hospital wards is to close is forced on politicians or public servants by changed demography. Some outside accidents or chance events, such as the Chernobyl nuclear melt-down, may also have a long term impact of an unpredictable nature. To an extent, therefore, policy decisions represent reactions to outside pressures.

Of course, Ireland is not simply a recipient of outside influences, important though they are. Even in relation to multinational investment, public bodies – such as the Industrial Development Authority – examine, encourage, promote and decline offers of commercial developments. Increasingly, misgivings about the environmental impact of proposed investments are cited when foreign companies are spurned. Nevertheless, most of the time, the Republic's economy is open to outside as well as domestic investment initiatives. Many decisions in Irish public policy are in effect conditioned by this reality.

### 'Great man' policy-making

To recognise the importance of outside influence is not to ignore autonomous Irish action. Not everyone would see the Republic's current economic status or its social policies as primarily predetermined. For example, Ireland did not *have* to borrow money to support public spending when the oil crisis of the mid-1970s radically upset the world economy. The role of Irish actors must therefore be assessed. The shift of emphasis in Ireland's political and social policies since the late 1950s is popularly explained by the impact of a senior civil servant, T. K. Whitaker, and the then Taoiseach, Seán Lemass. The two men are credited with formulating, popularising and forming a coalition of support for a dramatic policy with new laws, innovative institutions and fresh thinking about economics, planning and development.

'Great men' do, therefore, have some impact on the policy process, but their scope for innovation is limited by important political, economic and social considerations. Lemass, for example, had been a senior minister for many years in administrations of a conservative and protectionist kind. His espousal of radical measures on free trade, planning and Northern Ireland must be seen in the light of economic crisis, high emigration and pressure on his party's popularity. Fianna Fáil needed to react to the symptoms of a national malaise that threatened its legitimacy as 'the national party'. Further, Lemass' ideas drew directly on European and Christian social principles. His administrations were, in part, the Irish vehicle for a European-wide set of ideas fashionable among Christian Democrats. Whitaker was only one of a group of civil servants challenging the received wisdom of his civil service department.

The policy process is an interaction between ideas, social and political pressures, and opportunity in the context of the world economic order. The popularity of the 'great man' explanation of the policy process arises from the simplification and dramatisation it allows in our understanding of events. In fact the process is far more mundane, complex and unsatisfactory. It involves many people and agencies marching to tunes of self-interest, with remarkably little common purpose. In Ireland, most of the important participants in the making of major national decisions belong to the higher levels of the government bureaucracy, economic pressure groups, major companies and senior politicians.

### 'Professionals' and the bureaucracy

The number of people involved in policy-making at the highest level may actually be less than 500. The assertion earlier that policy is what government does, should, however, alert us to the significance of decisions made, and discretion exercised, by even the lowliest public official. Formal declarations of non-discrimination against travelling people, for example, are not real descriptions of policy if Gardaí regularly harass such people, or housing offices routinely ignore their plight. The beef tribunal which reported in 1994 looked into allegations of irregularities under the Export Credit Guarantee Insurance Scheme in respect of beef exports in the 1987-88 period. In doing so, it highlighted major gaps between formal policy and administrative practice.

The government bureaucracy includes many public servants who prefer to be seen as professionals rather than bureaucrats. 'Professionals' frequently claim that their judgements are based on abstract and neutral ideas, and are to that extent non-political. Thus, health policy relies in part on the pattern of priorities advocated by health board doctors, and not just on instructions from the Department of Health. When questioned about their decisions, doctors regularly talk of 'clinical judgement'. The scarce resources that they command – like medicines and operating theatres – should, it is thus claimed, be outside the public arena, because a doctor's priorities can only be judged by his or her peers. Though their use of resources for one treatment may deny them for another, doctors, like engineers and other professionals, would not regard themselves as part of a *political* process. Further, though governments set the total spending limits, the precise allocation of funds to different hospitals and specialisms has been devolved to local health board members. Health policy is, therefore, significantly influenced by boards of councillors, by medical and paramedical professionals, and by ministerial appointees.

## Departments and their civil servants

In this chapter we will be concentrating on major decisions. In Ireland, these are largely the outcome of initiatives taken within government departments. Where legislation is required to enforce new policies, this is secured by the government's majority in the legislature. All the main parties run on tightly authoritarian lines, and Irish governments can almost always retain control, despite small majorities – or even in a minority – if the opposition is divided.

---

**Major government departments**

Department of An Taoiseach
Department of An Tánaiste
Department of Finance (Deputy Prime Minister)
Department of Agriculture, Food and Forestry
Department of the Arts, Culture and the Gaeltacht
Department of Defence
Department of Education
Department of Enterprise & Employment
Department of the Environment
Department of Equality & Law Reform
Department of Foreign Affairs
Department of Health
Department of Justice
Department of the Marine
Department of Social Welfare
Department of Tourism & Trade
Department of Transport, Energy & Communications

---

Government departments are organised on functional lines to cover the major areas of policy such as agriculture, health and foreign affairs.

The administrative cost of running departments, as opposed to expenditure on the provision of the services for which they are responsible, is about 10 per cent of total government spending. There are over thirty departments, or equivalents, but the Department of Finance occupies a key position, as the custodian of government money. Each department is staffed by civil servants, the most senior of whom is called the Secretary. Departmental Secretaries, their Assistant Secretaries and Principals are the most powerful public servants in the government bureaucracy. Their ideas of what is desirable, possible and, to a degree, politically advantageous for the government, are most influential in deciding what is done. The Secretaries are the main channels of civil service advice available to ministers and, though ministers frequently change, their advisers do not. Because of their influence, much attention had been focused by critics on what is claimed to be their lack of social vision and openness to new ideas. Such comments have often centred on their supposedly narrow educational background and their cautious outlook, encouraged by slow promotion and lack experience of work in the private sector.

All but one of the twenty-five Secretaries in 1996 were men. They normally hold office for a maximum of seven years. Some observers have suggested that continuation in their appointments should be linked to their performance. In this way Secretaries would have an extra incentive to impose more accountable management systems on their departments. Traditionally, once appointed Secretaries were very secure in their posts. Secretaries' career paths have typically been entirely in the civil service. Though the top posts are now open to wider competition, *de facto* most appointments are by internal promotion.

Those on the senior ranks below Secretary may have entered the service after university, but still at a junior grade. Civil servants themselves see that the hierarchical system has some dampening effect on initiative but feel that caution, even parsimony, is a virtue in a servant of the public. Though some management techniques may have been learned from the private sector, the civil servants' view of the world is distinctive. Public service, in the opinion of senior civil servants, remains a bastion of integrity, national responsibility and hard work, which bears laudable comparison with other sectors of Irish public life. As the Secretary of the Department of the Taioseach put it:

> I am proud that the Irish civil service . . . has a record in providing quality services that compares well with the civil services of other countries . . . and with any of the private organisations I have encountered.[1]

It is indeed difficult to argue with such a view. It may be, however, that this self-image makes senior civil servants somewhat unresponsive to new ideas from business, academia, pressure groups and elsewhere.

### Parties and policy-making – sidelining the civil service?

The exact list of tasks carried out by, and the title of, each government department varies with changing political fashion, administrative convenience and government responsibilities. There remains, however, a fairly identifiable core of departments which have been involved with agriculture, defence, education, local government, foreign affairs and other major areas since the early years of the state. It would be odd if, as individuals and collectively, public officials who worked in these areas did not develop coherent and generalised views of where the public interest lies. Even modest, self-effacing civil servants would presumably make at least some effort to resist serious challenges to the 'departmental line' from their nominal superiors – government ministers. Of course, ministers ultimately have to prevail if open clashes of opinion occur. Plainly, senior politicians also have their own ideas about public priorities, particularly in relation to major policy initiatives.

When a single party forms a government, its ideas may be fairly broad and open to change through cabinet reconsideration and civil service advice. In a coalition, however, some distinct policy ideas may have been decided by prior negotiation between the parties. Subsequent civil service reservations may therefore count for little. To ensure a coalition survives, individual ministers may view it as their primary task to 'deliver' on a policy promise, despite reservations from within their own party or department. When the 1973 Fine Gael–Labour coalition was formed, several Labour ministers appointed advisers from outside the civil service to provide them with non-departmental advice. This practice has since been adopted in varying degrees by subsequent governments.

Since 1992, new coalition governments have also appointed

'programme managers', generally from outside the civil service, to monitor the achievement of agreed policy objectives. These managers meet weekly before cabinet meetings, and fulfil a valuable coordinating role between departments. Despite early reservations, most senior civil servants now see the managers, generally one per minister, as an asset. In particular, they help keep the minister in touch with party political opinion, with other ministers and with outside interests; and they are considered to be especially valuable in departments with a reforming agenda. In opposition, Fine Gael was critical of the role of advisers to the Fianna Fáil–Labour government. Nevertheless, the system was continued by John Bruton as Taoiseach. Indeed, the programme managers are credited with ensuring the relatively low level of friction in the three-party government, despite its broad ideological span. Since programme managers and other political advisers are essentially the personal appointees of ministers, they forfeit their appointments when their ministers leave office. Despite the fairly general approval which these 'outsiders' now enjoy, for most of the time the policy process is still dominated by civil servants acting within the broad parameters set by the government of the day.

### 'The minister requests . . .'

The better a party's preparations while in opposition, or the more specific its proposals, the smaller the role civil servants play in policy formulation. Formally, and importantly in legal terms, the orders, advice and publicly expressed opinions of civil servants are all in the name of the minister. Under the Ministers and Secretaries Act 1924 the minister is the 'corporation sole' of the department. All legal powers are conferred on him or her, and used in his or her name. Thus phrases such as 'I am instructed by the minister to . . .' or 'the minister requests . . .' appear on documents that the minister may never have seen, or of which he or she is only vaguely aware.

Since the same formal language also appears when the minister is showing a direct personal interest in an area of policy, to the outsider the authority of the document is the same. Senior civil servants communicate not only for their minister by letter but also informally through networks of contacts in every aspect of public life. A retired Secretary to the Department of Finance has written:

> Only those who have worked close to Ministers have any idea of the many demands on their time. One indication of the limited amount of time which a Minister can devote to the affairs of his Department is the difficulty which the official head of the Department (the Secretary) and his senior colleagues experience in obtaining a meeting with him. Perhaps this difficulty is accentuated in the Department of Finance, whose Minister is subject to unusually varied pressures; it is certainly not a problem of personalities since the difficulty does not vary much with different Ministers.[2]

As they do not personally build houses, teach children or manufacture goods, civil servants must keep a check on public policy by monitoring those who do. Information is crucial and the skill of interpreting it central to the civil servants' role. For this reason their work is dominated by a stream of official figures, reports from their juniors, personal impressions, politicians' and citizens' letters, gossip and media speculation. Their centrality in these networks of information is both a strength and a source of vulnerability for civil servants. How do they make sense of it all? The model of the world they employ is a vitally important element in how policy is formed and reformed. This is why the departmental line, the civil servants' backgrounds and the openness to fresh ideas are important.

### Keeping track of policy

There is a constitutional limit of fifteen on the number of cabinet ministers and they may be assisted by up to seventeen ministers of state. All must be members of the Oireachtas (two may be from the Seanad). To form an idea of how difficult it is for ministers to keep track of the areas of policy for which they are responsible, it is useful to look at the structure of even a small department. The primary functions of the Department of

Foreign Affairs are to advise the government on Ireland's external relations, to be a channel for official communications with
foreign governments and international agencies; and to monitor
developments in Northern Ireland. European Union business is
a significant burden for the department. Yet despite all this, its
running costs, at home and abroad, account for less than half of
1 per cent of total government expenditure. About 130 people
above the level of Third Secretary are based in headquarters in
Dublin. Several hundred more employees, many of them not
Irish, are dispersed in various forms of official representation
around the world. In 1996 there were over forty separate
embassies, consulates and their equivalents.

It would be unreasonable to expect ministers to be *au fait* with
all of their departments' work. Nevertheless, any task is liable to
become the focus of public controversy. Thus, for example, the
routine issuing of passports, to which few ministers had given
much attention, became a political embarrassment in 1987,
when irregularities were discovered to be occurring at the Irish
Embassy in London. Although these seemed to be attributable to
a specific civil servant, the Minister for Foreign Affairs was called
on to give an account of how such a situation 'was allowed to
happen'.

More important for policy-making is the rivalry that exists
between departments. Thus, to take another Foreign Affairs
example, EU matters have been the responsibility of that department since the negotiations for Ireland's entry in 1973.
Nevertheless, the department's views, tutored by the exigencies
of diplomacy, can only be brought to fruition if they prevail over
the possibly conflicting views of those responsible for finance
and agriculture. To some extent, departments 'capture' areas of
discretion or advice. If responsibility is given to another department, control over the flow of information, prestige and power
are lost. Thus there might just be conflict between the
Department of Foreign Affairs and the Department of Enterprise
and Employment in regard to negotiations on trade treaties with
foreign governments or international organisations.

In many government departments it is difficult to assess the impact of policy other than in terms of increased service provision. Whether, as a consequence, Ireland is better educated, defended, housed or provided for in terms of health and welfare is difficult to gauge. A reasonable measure may, however, be what is spent on these services. Thus civil servants who come to identify an increase in their service with the general national good, may be motivated to maximise their departmental budgets. Such motives, with the understandable personal interest in more salary, promotion and prestige have, according to their critics, become significant reasons for the seemingly inexorable growth of public expenditure.

### Odium or plaudits for the minister?

Although politicians in government are only directly involved in a small proportion of the policy for which they are 'responsible', that proportion is often the most controversial. The public odium that attends failure, or indeed insensitivity in policy implementation, descends on the politicians in office. Cabinet ministers are especially vulnerable to criticism. By contrast, they must also be seen to receive the plaudits for policy successes and popular initiatives. There are few more prized opportunities for a politician than the opening of a factory, a new road or a hospital in or near his or her constituency. A department that fails to alert its minister to a possibly embarrassing development, or to a potential opportunity to be associated with a success, would be open to sharp criticism. On the other hand, departments rely on their ministers to secure their position in the interdepartmental rivalry on policies and responsibilities. To a civil service department, a good minister wins winnable battles in cabinet or elsewhere, makes decisions on the files sent to him or her, and stands up for the officials in times of criticism. For a minister, a good department is one where the opportunities for good publicity are substantial. Briefly, if the public mood is sympathetic, a minister may even gain in popularity by being seen to take 'unpopular' decisions. The public tolerance for cutbacks is short, however.

## Policy or administration?

The supposed dichotomy between policy and administration is one to which civil servants often point. They claim that, once broad and clearly political choices are made by ministers, they merely facilitate their implementation. To this extent civil servants are politically neutral administrators, while politicians are the effective policy-makers. This model of the policy process is rather like the legal description. Many analysts of the policy process recognise it to be of limited use, but it remains a powerful ideal. Attempts have been made, therefore, to create a distinct policy-making section within each government department, called the 'aireacht', to secure the clearer identification and separation of functions. The thinking is that those not in this small and senior group could then develop systems of administration free of 'political' considerations.

The aireacht idea was first put forward in 1969 and was to a large extent cold-shouldered by both civil servants and politicians at the time. Nevertheless, the model has been influential, particularly with official and other would-be reformers of the current system. Most departments now have specialist units for planning, finance, organisation and personnel. Basic to the reformers' views is the idea that better policy would be made by politicians and senior officials who were freed from day-to-day responsibility for administration per se. This approach received important support with the publication in September 1985 of the White Paper, *Serving the Country Better:*

> There are, in fact, two broad functions which the civil service performs: the delivery of a wide range of services to the public; and the formulation of policy, and advice and planning on behalf of Government. . . . In most departments there is no clear or satisfactory separation between policy advisory functions and the day-to-day management of executive activities. As long as this remains so, there will not be sufficient emphasis either on the managerial concern with getting results, reducing costs and improving the service to the public or on the development of corporate planning and long term policy analysis. [3]

Despite this endorsement, the 1985 White Paper has not been followed by any significant change in the pattern of civil service organisation of day-to-day work. Even so, *Delivering Better Government*, published in May 1996, repeats much of the analysis of 1969 and 1985. This report was prepared by seven departmental secretaries and two other senior civil servants. It was heavily influenced by the new paradigm of 'public management', and the particular experiences of New Zealand and Australia. Those who use public services, for example, are called 'customers' rather than citizens. *Delivering Better Government* is subtitled 'A Programme of Change for the Irish Civil Service'. At its launch the Taoiseach, John Bruton, described the programme as a central part of the government's Strategic Management Initiative (SMI): a major review of public management practice.

### Improving financial planning and budgetary management

The SMI was set up in 1994. It recognises that the efficiency of the public sector is a vital part of Ireland's national competitiveness in the global market. It is possible, therefore, that the reform proposals of 1996 will have more impact than their predecessors. Already, under the SMI, each department has had to set out its objectives, strategies and produce other management plans.

One specific aim of *Delivering Better Government* is to change financial planning by government departments from a year-to-year to a three-year basis. Most areas of policy-making are overshadowed by the formulation of the government's annual budgetary proposals, though the timetable for completing the budget may be affected by elections or other political crises. Typically, however, each summer, government departments prepare their plans for the year beginning the following January. These plans will concern spending increases or cuts, both on the current and capital accounts. Each department's plans reflect its priorities, either as enunciated by its ministers or put forward by civil servants themselves. Often new ideas may have been formulated in the department for some time in the hope that a 'sympathetic' minister will adopt them.

Broadly, one year's departmental budget was very similar to the previous year's, with changes confined to small adjustments to established services, and only a few new departures. For although the budgetary process is an annual one, many aspects are legally or politically committed for a longer period, so change was for long confined to a small proportion of actual expenditure. Most attention is given to new items, by the Department of Finance to begin with, and then by ministers – first in a cabinet subcommittee, and finally in full cabinet. The pattern of incremental change was, however, radically altered by the Fianna Fáil government in 1987.

Departments with large budgets, such as education and health, were obliged to make sweeping economies. These involved the abandonment of previously safe projects and the loss of health service and teaching jobs. For example, in 1988 the Minister for Health set a target of 2,000 health service redundancies. Though the public finances were improving, a similar programme of cuts was set out for 1989; but this time social welfare and local government suffered most. Since 1987, in order to accomplish such economies, the annual budgetary process begins with a policy review – involving ministers, senior civil servants and a private sector economist – which sets the targets within which departments must operate. The impact of all this was to reduce government expenditure from 53 per cent of GDP in 1986 to 41 per cent in 1991.

In 1996 the budgeting system moved on to a multi-annual framework. Departments must set out the cost of continuing policies for next year, and then for the subsequent two years on a 'no-policy-change' basis. In effect, departments are being obliged to signal the cost of policy changes much more clearly. The new system will thus call for greater budgetary discipline from civil servants. It may, on the other hand, be even tougher on politicians, because it will make it more difficult to effect changes in the short term.

Civil service running costs were already being budgeted on a similar three-year basis. For two cycles prior to 1996 there were Three Year Administration Budget Agreements between the Minister for Finance and ministers responsible for line departments. The agreements, however, did not cover major programmes so were a relatively small part of the government's expenditure. Under the agreements, departments enjoyed a degree of freedom to adjust their spending on training, administration, publicity and the like, from year to year without Department of Finance approval.

Such tight budgeting involved severe competition for funds and intense competition between sections within each department. The major rows, however, have usually been between spending departments and the Department of Finance, and these take place during the autumn months, when detailed submissions are considered. The Department of Finance aggregates the figures and compares them with the government's capacity to raise taxes or borrow money at home or abroad. Inevitably the department seeks to reduce expenditure by questioning the need for, the details of, or the costings associated with, each department's proposals. After the haggling is over, the Department of Finance publishes details of the proposed expenditure in January. The Minister for Finance then prepares his own budgetary proposals that outline how the government intends to raise the money to meet its bills.

In assessing the level of taxation, the Department of Finance works closely with the Revenue Commissioners who are responsible for its collection. The Dáil discusses the government's plans, but only rarely are changes made before the necessary legislation is passed. Once the cabinet and civil servants, working in confidence, have arrived at a pattern of expenditure and taxation – involving intense bargaining and compromise – it would be difficult to find room for significant adjustments.

Further, for a government to be unsuccessful in carrying its budget in a Dáil vote is a cause of serious political embarrassment. By convention, such a defeat leads to a general election. Major changes in the budget have been forced in the past, especially when the disposition of forces in the Dáil has been problematic. Deputies have imposed significant adjustments on both single-party Fianna Fáil and on coalition governments' budget proposals, notably in respect of taxation affecting farmers. In 1987 the minority Fine Gael government was defeated on its budget, over the imposition of value added tax on children's apparel, and subsequently lost office. It remains the case, nevertheless, that major changes to a government's proposals are very infrequent.

The annual budgetary cycle is completed when each department's accounts are audited by the Comptroller and Auditor-General (C & A-G) and his or her staff. The Dáil's Public Accounts Committee goes through the C & A-G's report in great detail with the 'accounting officer' (usually the Secretary) of each department. The committee is generally chaired by an opposition deputy, as a defence against accusations of favouritism for the government party or parties. Following legislation in 1993, the C & A-G's reports now also cover the 'value for money' being given by government departments and other public agencies.

However, the budgetary process places an emphasis on several crucial annual deadlines and/or meetings at which decisions are finalised. Thus, policy-makers can themselves become overly concerned with their ability to defend their proposals in the short term. Most of the government's expenditure is, however, committed on a continuing basis, so considerable attention is paid to those budget items that can be adjusted quickly. This means that some kinds of expenditure are especially vulnerable to change for *ad hoc*, short term reasons, and this may lead to serious misallocation of scarce public resources. It is this 'short termism' that the new multi-year budgetary framework is intended to reduce.

Since December 1990, the autonomous National Management Agency, staffed by non-civil servants, has been responsible for raising the funds necessary to finance the government's borrowing requirements and for management of the national debt. The agency is formally responsible to the Minister for Finance, who is also its accounting officer. Remarkably, it is claimed that the loss of responsibility for managing the national debt has not significantly reduced the power of the Department of Finance, and it continues to regulate the finances of all other departments, as well as borrowing by other state bodies.

### Uno duce, una voce

The Department of Finance's dominating position in the budgetary process is only part of the reason for its influence. The department, which is the only one mentioned in the Constitution, is involved in all aspects of economic policy and planning. It negotiates Ireland's trade agreements (though this is now largely a role for the EU) and it has responsibility for monetary and banking policy and the like. It does, however, have rivals. The Department of the Taoiseach is an increasingly important part of the policy-making process.

The Taoiseach has been a most influential policy-maker from the beginning. He is, after all, the leader of the main government party, and is able to choose his colleagues in government – even though this power is somewhat diminished under a coalition arrangement. It is to him that the public look to champion the government's cause and offer leadership. Until 1982, the Taoiseach's Department remained small, and essentially 'non-interventionist'. Under recent holders of the post, however, the department has grown in size, and so too has the scope of its direct responsibility. It provides policy and administrative support on a variety of issues to other departments, depending on the Taoiseach's priorities and, unlike other departments, it does not have a statutorily defined area of responsibility. Significantly for reform of the policy process, the department has responsibility for the promotion of the SMI.

The Taoiseach, like other ministers, may appoint special advisers with a party political background. The Department of the Taoiseach also has a number of junior ministers – or 'Ministers of State' – attached to it, including the government Chief Whip. Thus, the Taoiseach's team has a crucial hold on the legislative programme and on party discipline. Especially under single party governments, the Taoiseach has been able to exercise both forceful leadership and close management of the government's overall business. The Department of the Taoiseach is potentially the most powerful department of all: the firm leadership style of one recent Taoiseach, Charles Haughey, led to the Italian phrase, *Uno duce, una voce!* (One leader, one voice!), entering everyday Irish political parlance.

The role of the Taoiseach as Ireland's representative at the European Council has added to the centrality of his department. Yet the Department of Foreign Affairs has also gained prominence as a consequence of Ireland's EU membership. Ireland's permanent representation in Brussels is dominated by Foreign Affairs, although other departments, particularly agriculture, are well represented. Because many policies have their origins in the European Commission, a close watching brief is kept, and representations made, by Irish civil servants based in Brussels.

### Radical change – an impossibility?

The budgetary process, with its tendency to encourage piecemeal and incremental change, departmental rivalry, civil service conservatism and caution, acts as a barrier to the establishment of radically new public policies. Despite the rhetoric of party politics, in Ireland as elsewhere, public policies are more notable for continuity than for change. New ideas take time to find acceptance among politicians, bureaucrats and the public – and even longer to affect state provision. Small countries like Ireland often wait to learn from experiment and innovation elsewhere; and in Ireland's case the example of the UK is inevitably a powerful influence. Be that as it may, there has been serious effort recently to cast the net wider when looking for new ideas.

Some policies have not changed in broad principles since independence. Most notably, the social welfare system, which accounts for nearly 30 per cent of current government spending, developed piecemeal, with no serious review until 1986. Major commissioned reports, on areas such as taxation or public sector management, do provide a vehicle for new ideas; but their influence is ultimately constrained by party and bureaucratic politics, as well as by the lack of broad public interest, still less consensus. The same is true of policy ideas arising from less elaborate forms of consultation and advice – of the kind submitted to government by private and semi-official bodies such as the National Economic and Social Council (NESC).

The NESC was established in 1973 specifically to provide a channel for advice to government, through the Taoiseach, from employers and trade unions in particular. The NECS's chairperson is the Secretary of the Department of the Taoiseach. It has, therefore, better access than most pressure groups, but the government does receive policy representation from a broad range of sources. Some reports, books and memoranda have been influential and have marked turning-points in particular areas of policy; others have helped change the general climate of opinion about particular policies. Critics maintain, however, that Irish policy-makers – whether politicians or civil servants – are not sufficiently open to new ideas. Only when they come from powerful pressure groups, such as the major producer organisations, are they regularly influential.

### State-sponsored industries

A main plank in the agenda of the nationalist movement in Ireland was to control market conditions and build up Irish industry. As we have seen, this was Fianna Fáil's main economic strategy. Thus, when it took office in 1932, tariffs were placed on imports to encourage Irish entrepreneurs to set up manufacturing businesses. This policy certainly helped to widen the Irish manufacturing base by protecting it from outside competition. Reliance on the domestic market, however, kept industrial concerns relatively small scale and uncompetitive in international markets. Moreover, there were also essential economic and service functions which did not attract private investment. In these cases successive governments, none of which had any particular ideological preference for state industry, did not hesitate to established semi-autonomous state-sponsored bodies to perform them.

Examples include the Electricity Supply Board (ESB), Coras Iompar Eireann (CIE, the public transport authority), Bord na Móna (the peat development agency), Aer Lingus (the national airline), Telecom Eireann (the state telecommunications company) and Bord Gáis Eireann (the Irish gas board). The commercial state-sponsored bodies operate like private companies in that they are expected to make profits to cover their operations and expansion. However, this has been a particular problem for the two transport undertakings. Despite the splitting up of CIE into separate railway, 'country'-bus and Dublin-bus divisions, and the introduction of experienced private sector management, a continuation of government subsidies has been necessary to ensure that it remains viable. Aer Lingus too had its problems in the early 1990s, and only just survived as a consequence of an EU-approved subvention from public funds. That the EU had an input into the decision-making in this case is a reminder that the state-sponsored sector in Ireland is likely to be transformed before the end of the century. EU anti-monopoly and free-competition legislation will present the ESB and Telecom Eireann with special challenges; these companies have already shed thousands of workers in an effort to meet them.

Be that as it may, the 100 or so state-sponsored bodies still employ almost 75,000 people, about a third of the public service. The heads of these larger semi-state or state-sponsored bodies have a clear and direct role in public policy. They have open communications with ministers and senior civil servants in their 'parent' departments. As commercial enterprises, they also invest large sums of money in important infrastructural projects, and the government takes a close interest in all their plans. Indeed, the government itself appoints the directors and board or council members who make up the management bodies of state-sponsored companies.

The political importance of some of these companies arises from their dependence on public funding; the significance of others, especially those promoting economic development, comes from their influence on the key function of job creation. After a 1994 rationalisation of industrial promotion activities, several bodies now share this responsibility: Bord Fáilte is the Irish Tourist Board; Forbairt has responsibility for encouraging indigenous industry; the Industrial Development Authority (IDA-Ireland) is charged with attracting investment from abroad; the Shannon Free Airport Development Company (SFADCO) and Udarás Na Gaeltachta (an authority for the Irish-speaking regions) promote investment in their own particular areas; and Forfás (the policy and advisory board for industrial development) has a coordinating role among these and other agencies with employment generation roles. To an extent all these compete with one other to develop plans, secure investment and influence government policy.

## Legislators and policy-making

The role of legislators in the policy process in parliamentary systems is in practice rather restricted. Ireland is certainly no exception. The executive branch, the government, controls the Dáil by party discipline, by the generation of legislation, by the allocation of parliamentary time and, not least, by the control of information. Only at times of intense public excitement, such as the fall of the Reynolds-led government in 1994, is the Dáil central to policy-making. In such periods, the televised debates of Dáil proceedings become the focus of public interest. Generally, however, the main action is taking place elsewhere.

To redress the imbalance of power between the executive and the legislature somewhat, the Oireachtas has sought to strengthen its committee system. A fillip to this project came from the inadequacy of accountability highlighted by alleged financial scandals involving the state-sponsored bodies in 1991, and the beef industry in 1992. Clearly Dáil methods for obtaining information from ministers and/or civil servants were hopelessly inadequate. In 1993, therefore, the Dáil committee system was overhauled and new standing committees established. These bodies are better resourced than those which preceded them, and the backbench deputy in the chair is paid for his or her pains. The committees can summon senior public servants to give evidence, though there has been some resistance by civil servants when called. Indeed, in July 1995 the Garda Commissioner (or Chief of Police) bluntly refused a summons to come before the Oireachtas Joint Committee on the Family to discuss the way the Gardaí were dealing with the drugs problem.

Ministers must also discuss their plans with legislative committees, and the committees themselves can initiate legislation. The Dáil may thus be able to increase its role in the policy process in the future, but several important barriers remain. Deputies and senators may find the burdens of constituency business, local authority membership and party duties leave insufficient time for the committee work. The government is likely to be more parsimonious with support services than deputies would wish. Further, though parliamentarians enjoy privilege against libel for what they say, witnesses and the reporting media do not. As a result, the committee process may be inhibited somewhat. Finally, the government parties have retained a majority on each of the twenty-one committees as well as holding the chair of most of them. It may not, therefore, be in the committees' interests to be too disruptive.

The investigative powers of the Dáil are augmented by the office of the Ombudsman. The Ombudsman has the power to investigate the actions of government departments, local authorities and the postal and telecommunications service. Besides annual reports to the Dáil, the Ombudsman is free to make special reports at any time. But these reports address individual complaints of poor public service rather than broad policy – because the Ombudsman's role is limited to monitoring and promoting administrative accountability. In 1996 the Constitutional Review Group called for the Ombudsman's office to be strengthened, possibly by means of a new article in the Constitution. Meanwhile, new legislation on freedom of information and the Ombudsman's regulatory powers may eventually bring the office in from the margins of the policy process.

## Conclusion

In this chapter, we have seen that public policy is constrained by private interests and commercial realities, which are largely shaped by Ireland's place in the world economic order. Demographic, climatic and environmental factors also have a role in determining what governments do. Within these constraints, and despite the increasing importance of the EU in policy-making, Ireland does have important decisions of its own to make. To the extent that the political system has autonomy, powerful figures in public life can make a significant impact, given the political and economic opportunity. However, far too much emphasis is placed on the explanatory value of the activity of 'great persons'.

The making of Irish public policy is dominated by a relatively small number of politicians and high-level civil servants. The process is often an incremental and annual one, though there have been some radical turning-points. Economic policy, taxation and government expenditure are central to the concerns of all recent Irish governments. On these issues there is a remarkably broad consensus among the politicians and in the civil service. On most policies, therefore, the bureaucrats are very influential. Politicians ultimately take public responsibility and their attention to policy is greatest when either controversy and/or specific political commitments are high.

## Notes

1 *Administration*, Vol. 30, No. 4, 1980, pp. 53-4.
2 *Ibid.*
3 *Serving the Country Better*, Dublin: Stationery Office, 1985, pp. 5-6.

## Further reading

J. Coakley and Michael Gallagher (eds), *Politics in the Republic of Ireland*, (2nd edition), Dublin: Folens, 1993.

S. Dooney and J. O'Toole, *Irish Government Today*, Dublin: Gill & Macmillan, 1991.

J. Lee, *Ireland 1912-1985: Politics and Society*, Cambridge: Cambridge University Press, 1989.

## 5

# The Constitution and the law

The present Constitution, Bunreacht na hEireann, came into operation on 29 December 1937. Its fiftieth anniversary in 1987 renewed the debate about what it should contain and how frequently it should be reviewed. Since then there have been several important constitutional changes, arising both from amendments and from judicial interpretation. Moreover, the Constitution is now more than ever a focus for attention from political parties and pressure groups. In 1995 a Constitutional Review Group, chaired by former senior civil servant T. K. Whitaker, was set up to determine whether modifications were needed, and what these might be. Its report, published in July 1996, will provide the basis for a continuing debate on changes to Bunreacht na hEireann. This chapter looks at the provisions of the Constitution, its origins and the wider system of law of which it is a part.

## The Constitution

The principles of liberal democracy were fashioned and tested by the French and American revolutions at the end of the eighteenth century. The rule of law and the pivotal position of the Constitution are of utmost importance in this system of government. Liberal democratic theory grew up in reaction to the rule of the many by the few. At its base was the notion of 'individual liberty'. For liberal democratic theorists, the power of government comes from the people, and they wished to see government representing the will of its people, through consultation, election and plebiscite. It was also realised that if tyranny by a minority could exist, then so too could the tyranny of a majority. The freedom of the individual had to be guaranteed, therefore; and an agreed set of rules and standards, to be used as an objective test of the protection given to individuals against the government, was established under the concept of 'the rule of law'. The essential basis of this law was the written constitution.

---

**What is a Constitution for?**

A Constitution does several things:
- It outlines the structure of government. The liberal democratic form of government is distinguished by the separation of the powers given to the legislature, the executive, and the judiciary.
- It reflects and codifies the values and beliefs of society.
- It is often a statement of intent – it presents an image of what the people would like their society to be. This is particularly so in countries experiencing great social or political upheaval.

---

Because the Constitution is the supreme source of law, it is usually made more difficult to change than other laws. Often the wording can only be altered when the people have been consulted by referendum. A Constitution is also usually open to judicial review. Thus, although the words cannot be changed by judges, the meaning of words, or the meaning of phrases, can – in effect, new rights and obligations can be created. Moreover, this process can sometimes produce an interpretation of the Constitution which is quite contrary to what was previously believed to be the case. This aspect of constitutional change will be looked at more closely below.

Newly independent countries frequently experience an initial period of relatively rapid constitutional change. This was the case with Ireland, which has had three Constitutions: one in 1919, another in 1922, and the present one in 1937. A further change of some constitutional importance was brought about by 1948 Republic of Ireland Act which, as the name suggests, made formal the status of the state as a republic.

## The first and second Constitutions

It is noteworthy that while the leaders of the Irish independence struggle were attempting to throw off British rule, their 1919 Constitution accepted the Westminster parliamentary system as a model for the new Irish government. Although the members of Sinn Féin asserted in principle and in practice their right to armed struggle, they were schooled in and accepted the ideals of constitutional politics. The Constitution of 1919 reflected the predominantly liberal-democratic nature of the independence movement, as well as the influence of Sinn Féin's legal advisers who were mostly trained in the British legal system.

The second Constitution, which was called the 'The Constitution of the Irish Free State', also followed the British model. It set up a bicameral legislature consisting of a lower house (Dáil) and an upper house (Seanad), with a cabinet government responsible to the Dáil. The Seanad consisted of members elected by a restricted franchise, and others appointed by the head of the government. There were some differences with Britain. Full adult suffrage was introduced, six years before Britain did so, and election by proportional representation was prescribed. Other important differences included measures to make the government more responsible to the people. There were provisions for the initiation of legislation from outside the Oireachtas, and for the calling of referendums to test public opinion on legislation. Following the example of the written constitutions of France and America, the Free State Constitution also included a declaration of rights. These included freedom of expression, religion and association, the principle of *habeas corpus*, and the inviolability of the citizen's home.

When Fianna Fáil was elected to government in 1932, it was clear that the Constitution would come under critical review, if only because it was based on the Anglo-Irish Treaty. De Valera intended to remove all vestiges of British control in Ireland from the Free State Constitution. The years between 1933 and the introduction of the new constitution in 1937 were used to get rid of what Fianna Fáil considered to be the most objectionable parts of the 1922 Constitution. The links with Britain were lessened, with the removal of the oath to the Crown and the virtual abolition of the office of Governor-General. In 1936, de Valera took advantage of the abdication of Edward VIII to remove any role for the British Crown from the Free State Constitution also. And in 1937 he finally introduced Bunreacht na hEireann, the third Irish Constitution.

## The tone of the 1937 Constitution

This Constitution plainly mirrored de Valera's views and represented a further break with Britain. 'In that Constitution', he later said, 'the traditional aspirations of our people, of national independence, national unity and the unfettered control of their domestic and foreign affairs have been set as the basic principles of the law by which we are to be governed.'[1]

The system of government specified was in the mould of that in numerous other liberal-democratic states: sovereignty lay with the people; the Head of State, the President, was to be elected; parliament was to consist of two houses; there would be a separate and independent judiciary. In addition, like some other written Constitutions, Bunreacht na hEireann contained an inventory of positive social principles; and it guaranteed certain individual rights. An obviously Roman Catholic ethos pervaded these provisions. In the articles on the family and its protection – especially the ban on divorce and the prescriptive attitude to the role of women as homemakers – the Constitution clearly reflected the pervasive Catholic teaching of the 1930s.

**The powers of the President**

- The President may refer any Bill to the Supreme Court to test whether it is constitutional. If a government wishes to proceed with a Bill declared repugnant to the Constitution, it must submit it to a referendum.
- A majority of the Seanad, and not less than one-third of TDs, may ask the President not to sign a Bill, because it is of such importance that the people should be consulted. It will then only be signed if approved by referendum, or by a new Dáil elected after a dissolution.
- The President may convene a meeting of the Houses of the Oireachtas; this is intended to cover the emergency situation where those whose job it is to call a meeting cannot, or will not.
- The Dáil is summoned and dissolved by the President, on the advice of the Taoiseach. If the Taoiseach has lost the support of the majority of TDs, the President may refuse a dissolution, giving the Dáil a chance to elect a different Taoiseach and avoid a general election.
- If the Dáil and government wish to restrict the time a Bill may be considered by the Seanad, the President must concur.
- The President may rule in a dispute between the Ceann Comhairle (the 'Speaker' of the Dáil) and the Seanad about whether a Bill is a 'money Bill', i.e., one in which the Seanad's role is very restricted.

**The President**

As Head of State, the President performs a range of formal acts of government as well as being the symbol of the state in ceremonial functions both at home and abroad. The Irish President is not the Head of Government, as in the USA or France – the Head of Government in Ireland is the Taoiseach. Nor is the Irish

President the source of governmental power, as is the British monarchy. De Valera claimed the President 'is there to guard the people's rights and mainly to guard the Constitution'. The President's role as representative of the people is signified by the provision that he or she be directly elected every seven years; and the President may be re-elected once only. On four occasions the main political parties have agreed on one candidate, and no election was necessary. Thus, for example, President Hillary re-nominated himself at the expiry of his first term of seven years in 1983 and was not opposed.

The last election was in November 1990, when Mary Robinson became the seventh President of Ireland. It is not at all certain that she will run for a second term in 1997.

There is little scope for the President to exercise other than negative power. The office has remained largely ceremonial and above controversy, and keeping Head of State above party politics or public contention was a priority for the Constitutional Review Group. Its report in 1996 called for little change in the powers and functions of the President. The only exception was that the President's power to refuse a dissolution of the Dáil should be replaced with a measure to allow a 'constructive vote of no confidence' by the Dáil. In effect, the Dáil would nominate an alternative Taoiseach and the President would not become embroiled in party political issues.

On one occasion, in 1976, the President actually resigned in order to ensure that the office did not become associated with political controversy. President O' Dálaigh, acting entirely properly in terms of the responsibilities of his office, referred the Emergency Powers Bill of the then Fine Gael/Labour government to the Supreme Court for a decision on its constitutionality. Although the Bill could not be declared unconstitutional, because the government had proclaimed a state of emergency, the President believed that the Court had the power nevertheless to inquire into the existence of a genuine state of emergency. Some government members were privately critical of this action, but there was little public concern about the matter. However, the Minister for Defence, Patrick Donegan, claimed that the

President was a 'thundering disgrace' because of his actions. President O' Dálaigh thought this 'outrageous criticism' had brought his office into disrepute, and the refusal of the Taoiseach to accept Donegan's resignation made it seem that he was standing by his minister's remarks. So the President resigned. Clearly he had been put in an impossible position by the government response. Moreover, the offence was compounded because the minister's remarks were made at an army function, and the supreme command of the defence forces is vested in the President.

President Robinson is herself a constitutional lawyer and has generally sought to enhance the role of head of state. Not surprisingly, therefore, she has exercised her powers more often than any of her predecessors. Indeed, of the nine Bills which were referred to the Supreme Court in the first six years of her presidency, four were found – at least in part – repugnant to the Constitution. President Robinson has also addressed both Houses of the Oireachtas in joint session more often than any previous holder of the office.

## The Seanad

The upper house, Seanad Eireann, has sixty members. It has a subordinate position in the Oireachtas. De Valera, effective author of Bunreacht na hEireann, felt the real value of the Seanad lay in checking, redrafting and amending legislation.

The Seanad's membership was originally intended to reflect the principle of 'vocationalism' (see Table 5.1). The idea that major interest groups ought to have parliamentary representation held great sway in Catholic and conservative movements in the 1930s.

Despite the ostensible vocationalism of the Seanad, in reality it soon became dominated as much by party politics as the lower house. This is hardly surprising, since eleven senators are nominated by the Taoiseach, while the electorate for the forty-three vocational members is made up of people already holding elected office themselves – members of the Oireachtas as well as

Table 5.1 *Vocational panels for Senate elections*

| Panel | Seats |
| --- | --- |
| Agriculture | 11 |
| Culture and Education | 5 |
| Industry and Commerce | 9 |
| Labour | 11 |
| Public Administration | 7 |

all county and county borough councillors. The final six senators are elected (three each) by the graduates of Trinity College (the University of Dublin) and the National University of Ireland. Within the enabling provisions of the Seventh Amendment of the Constitution, however, the arrangements for the election of these six senators may be revised. This must be a strong possibility, since there are two relatively new universities – the University of Limerick and Dublin City University – which are not represented.

The Seanad's powers are limited to revising and clarifying Bills, together with some minor constitutional duties and rights. It has no power of substance, especially in relation to financial matters. The Seanad is often used as a slow route out of politics for retiring TDs, or as a temporary political home for those who have failed to get re-elected. It has also been useful way for would-be TDs to make an initial entry on to the parliamentary scene. It is worthy of note that the Constitutional Review Group has suggested that consideration be given to the abolition of the Seanad.

### The Dáil and the government

According to the Constitution, the government will consist of not less than seven and not more than fifteen members. The Taoiseach, the Tánaiste (deputy prime minister) and the Minister for Finance must be members of the Dáil. All other members of the government must be members of the

Oireachtas, though only two can be from the Seanad. Ministers have the right to attend and to speak in either house. The government is responsible to the Dáil alone.

The lower house of the Oireachtas, Dáil Eireann, has varied in size from 128 seats to 166 at present. (There has to be one TD for every 20,000 to 30,000 electors.) The country is at present divided into 41 constituencies and their number must be revised at least once every 12 years to take account of population changes. The Dáil lasts for a maximum of 5 years. A general election must take place not later than 30 days after the dissolution and the newly elected Dáil must meet within 30 days from the polling date.

### The ministers of government

Usually each member of government becomes the head of one department of state, and sometimes of two. Apart from the members of government there can also be up to seventeen 'ministers of state', or junior ministers, who help their seniors in parliamentary and departmental duties. Although all ministers must be members of the Oireachtas, in practice they have almost always been members of the Dáil. A minister of state in the Department of the Taoiseach, with special responsibilities as government Chief Whip, attends government meetings as of right. In the Fine Gael/Labour/Democratic Left government formed in December 1994 it was agreed that an additional minister of state would also have a right to be present at cabinet meetings. The other ministers of state are occasionally invited to attend if an item within their particular area of responsibility warrants it.

The government has exclusive initiative in matters of finance. Article 17 of the Constitution states: 'Dáil Eireann may not pass any vote or resolution and no law shall be enacted for the appropriation of revenue or other public moneys, unless the purpose of the appropriation shall have been recommended to Dáil Eireann by a message from the Government signed by the Taoiseach.' As noted above, the power the Seanad has over

Table 5.2 *Constitutional referendums since 1937*

| Date | Subject |
| --- | --- |
| 1937 | Plebiscite to adopt the Constitution |
| 1959[a] | Introducing a new non-PR voting system |
| 1968[a] | Reducing the size of Dáil constituencies |
| 1968[a] | Introducing a new non-PR voting system |
| 1972 | Approving EU [EEC] membership |
| 1972 | Lowering the voting age from 21 to 18 |
| 1972 | Removing the 'special position' of the Roman Catholic Church |
| 1979 | Clarifying child adoption procedures |
| 1979 | Extending the graduate electorate for the Seanad |
| 1983 | Protecting the unborn – prohibition of abortion |
| 1984 | Extending voting rights to certain non-citizens |
| 1986[a] | Removing the prohibition on divorce |
| 1987 | Approving the Single European Act |
| 1992 | Approving the Maastricht Treaty |
| 1992[a] | Restricting the availability of abortion |
| 1992 | Guaranteeing a right to travel for abortion |
| 1992 | Guaranteeing a right to information on abortion |
| 1995 | Removing the prohibition on divorce |

*Note:*

[a] In these cases the proposition was defeated.

finances is highly limited: it may make recommendations but not substantive changes.

## Amendments to the Constitution

From 1941 until 1972 Bunreacht na hEireann remained unchanged. After an initial transitional period during which amendment was easier than it was later to be, Ireland's Constitution was essentially settled for over thirty years. It can only be changed by referendum, of which there have been several in recent years. In total since 1937 there have been fourteen amendments, including two passed before June 1941, which did not require popular approval (see Table 5.2).

## Judicial review

The provision for judicial review in Bunreacht na hEireann can be found at three points: Article 15.4.1 forbids the Oireachtas to pass any law repugnant to the Constitution; Article 34.3.2 gives the power of review to the High Court; and Article 34.3.3 allows the High Court's decisions on such questions to be appealed to the Supreme Court. The powers of the courts are, in this respect, greater than in some other liberal democracies; in particular, they can pronounce on the constitutionality of legislation both before and after it is passed. In the United States, by contrast, the courts can only rule on a piece of law *after* it has gone through the full legislative process. In France, courts can only rule on proposals *before* they become law. In the UK, broadly speaking, no review of constitutionality is permitted.

It is only relatively recently, however, that Bunreacht na hEireann has been changed through judicial interpretation – rather than by changes in its wording by means of referendums. From the 1960s onwards there was a growing realisation by Irish jurists, and others, of the way in which the Constitution provided legal guarantees as regards the fundamental rights of individuals. There are several reasons why such possibilities were not fully realised before then, and further reasons why the situation changed when it did:

- Until the mid-1960s, Irish lawyers were generally schooled in the British common law tradition. Britain does not have a written constitution and, in the absence of a Bill of Rights or its equivalent, relies on 'common law', or precedent, for the protection of the individual – against an attack upon his or her person, against the abuse of power by those set in authority, in defence of free speech, etc. There are, therefore, no defined reference points as regards the maintenance of social justice; and the sovereignty of parliament in the making of laws is considered absolute.
- The early years of Bunreacht na hEireann were dominated by the Second World War and internal subversion such as the IRA border campaign of the late 1950s. This was a period of

increased security legislation, the declaration of a state of emergency and, during the war, a standing military court. An atmosphere existed, therefore, which militated against the development of citizens' rights.
- That position changed in the 1960s. The security situation improved and emergency legislation was no longer required (although it remained on the statute book). More positively, Ireland's economic prosperity increased significantly in the 1960s, and higher living standards helped stem the flow of emigration. Consequently, the population became both younger and increasingly influenced by more cosmopolitan ideas.
- Further, there was change within the legal profession itself: standards of legal education improved; many students went to law schools in America and recognised the constitutional parallels between the USA and Ireland; new people began to dominate in the court structure; and by the early 1970s there was a majority of 'progressive' or 'liberal' judges in the Supreme Court. Judges became increasingly willing to reinterpret the Constitution, and more groups sought to pursue or protect their interests in this way.

**The consequences**

The main result of increasing judicial re-interpretation has been the augmentation of individual rights (see Table 5.3). Articles 40 to 44 of the Constitution list fundamental rights which 'the State guarantees in its laws to respect and, as far as practicable . . . to defend and vindicate' (Article 40.3.1).

It was decided by Justice Kenny in 1965 that the personal rights which may be invoked to invalidate legislation are not confined to those specified in Article 40. They also include all those rights which 'result from the Christian and democratic nature of the State'. Since this ruling, several rights unspecified in the Constitution have been recognised and enforced.

The Constitution has thus been developed by the 'implication' of rights – especially by reference to previously 'unused' sections

Table 5.3 *Citizens' rights in Ireland*

*Specified in Bunreacht na hEireann*
Equality before the law
Personal liberty
Privacy of the dwelling of every citizen
To express convictions and opinions freely
To assemble peaceably and without arms
To form associations and unions
Right to family, education, private property
Freedom of religion.

*Ruled by judicial interpretation to be implied**
To dispose of and withdraw one's labour
Not to belong to a trade union
To earn one's livelihood
The right to work
To litigate claims
To prepare for and follow a chosen career
To consult with, and be represented by, a lawyer when charged with a
    serious criminal offence
To be assisted by the state if one's health is in jeopardy
To marry
To free movement within the state

*Source:* A. J. Foley and S. Lalor (eds.), *Annotated Constitution of Ireland
1937–1994*, Dublin: Gill & Macmillan, 1995, *passim.*

– as well as by interpretation. Thus, for instance, the Preamble
was generally thought to be of little significance. It notes, *inter
alia*, that the people are: 'seeking to promote the common good,
with due observance of Prudence, Justice and Charity, so that the
dignity and freedom of the individual may be assured, true social
order attained, the unity of our country restored, and concord
established with other nations'. This has now been taken up by
the judiciary in order to keep the Constitution, and the law
flowing from it, in touch with prevailing ideas. Portentously
perhaps, it is to the Preamble and Articles 40 to 44 that the 1996
Constitutional Review Group suggested the most radical reword-
ing – to allow for *de facto* changes in society since the 1930s.

Several judgments by the Supreme Court have been won by individuals and groups seeking to restrain government action. Thus, for example, a member of the European Parliament, Patricia McKenna, succeeded in having the Supreme Court declare unconstitutional the use of public money by the government to fund its pro-divorce campaign before the 1995 referendum. Slightly out of the general run, the government took an action of the same kind to have reaffirmed a constitutional requirement which had effectively fallen into disuse. In 1992 the Attorney-General (the government's chief legal adviser) applied for and got a total ban on the disclosure of discussions which had taken place at any cabinet meeting in the past – on the grounds that the Constitution called for complete secrecy, even though cabinet proceedings had been the subject of informal press briefings for many years. Thus, words written in the 1930s which codified contemporary convention were used to reverse the more flexible practices of the 1990s.

## Ireland and European law

Another significant influence on the development of the Irish legal system has been the EU. The Constitution, as a product of Ireland's historical experience, emphasised the notion of sovereignty. An amendment to the Constitution was thus necessary to enable the Republic to become a full member of the EU, since membership involved some surrender of Irish sovereignty. This first 'European' amendment was approved by a large majority, and has been followed by two more. In December 1985 the then European Community adopted the Single European Act (SEA), intended to speed up and make more democratic its decision-making process; to be implemented, this was required to be ratified by each national parliament. In Ireland, however, there was a successful court challenge to the SEA, on the grounds that it was unconstitutional. In particular, the Supreme Court ruled that Title 111 of the SEA represented a surrender of sovereignty, and thus exceeded the normal constitutional power of an Irish government to conclude international agreements. The outcome was a second 'European' amendment, passed in 1987, which allowed Ireland to ratify the SEA. The third was passed in 1992, permitting ratification of the EU's Maastricht Treaty.

European Union law applies directly in member states to governments, companies and individuals. Its obligations, or the rights it establishes, must be upheld by national courts and then by the European Court of Justice. The European Union in effect, makes laws for Irish citizens, although they have not been passed by the Oireachtas. Irish ministers and MEPs are, of course, involved in the process of law-making at the EU level. There are five ways in which EU law can change or otherwise influence Irish law. The Council of Ministers and/or the European Commission can issue regulations, directives, decisions, recommendations and opinions. Regulations have direct effect in Ireland and require little or no domestic action. Directives are binding and may require a change in: (1) administrative practice; (2) secondary legislation in the form of ministerial orders called 'statutory instruments'; or, (3) amended or new legislation. Decisions from the Council and Commission are directly applicable and binding on the government, company or individual to whom they are addressed. The rest – recommendations and opinions – are not legally binding, though they may be considered politically so.

Irish courts are not allowed to review EU statutes, or their compatibility with the Constitution. Much domestic legislation is now a result of obligations placed on Ireland to conform with EU directives. But, until recently at any rate, the parliamentary supervision of EU law has been generally unsatisfactory, and debate on EU law has tended to be perfunctory. In March 1995 a Joint Committee on European Affairs was set up in the Oireachtas for the purpose of improving democratic accountability on EU matters. Despite that, many TDs and Senators still find little reward in attending to the detail of European legislation.

## Council of Europe: the European Court of Human Rights

The Council of Europe is made up of twenty-one West European parliamentary democracies. A further 'external' influence on the development of Ireland's legal system has been the Council's European Convention on Human Rights. An aggrieved citizen of a subscribing state, who has exhausted all domestic remedies, may petition the European Court of Human Rights in Strasbourg[1] for a ruling that his or her state has violated the rights guaranteed in the Human Rights Convention.[2] All EU members recognise the jurisdiction of the Court in Strasbourg in human rights cases.

The first major and direct influence of the European Court of Human Rights on the Irish system of justice was to establish that a petitioner must be free – in every sense – to seek redress before national courts. In the case in point, the court ruled that the expense of legal proceedings had put them outside the reach of the individual concerned. The result was that a form of legal aid provision in civil cases has had to be introduced in the Republic.

As we have already noted, a constitution is supposed to reflect and codify the values and beliefs of its society. Social values in Ireland, north and south, have generally been more conservative than elsewhere in Europe – especially as regards sexual behaviour. Partly as a consequence, in matters of individual rights, the law and Constitution remained less 'liberal' in Ireland for longer. Indeed, as many defenders of traditional values feared, the European Court has had a substantial impact in this respect. The first important decision arose from a case brought by a private citizen, Geoffrey Dudgeon, before the Northern Ireland courts in 1981, following a European judgment that homosexual activity between consenting adults should be permitted. Although the case was lost on a technicality, it was clear that the European Court ruling meant that the then legislation outlawing such behaviour – not only in Northern Ireland, but also in the Republic – violated a guaranteed right to privacy under the European Convention on human Rights.

The case increased the concern of those wishing to retain Ireland's less liberal laws that they might be changed 'from outside'. This anxiety was vividly displayed in the campaign for the Eighth Amendment (see below). In 1988 the European Court again showed its importance for Ireland, by upholding the claim of a Trinity College independent member of the Seanad, David Norris, that his rights were infringed by the criminal law on homosexuality. To meet the requirements of the *Norris* judgment, in 1993 the government introduced new legislation on homosexual behaviour – replacing the then existing British-made laws which dated back to 1861 and 1865.

Ireland signed the European Convention on Human Rights in 1953. It accepted the idea of compulsory implementation, as well as the legislation that followed from Court judgments. The process of obtaining a judgment is, however, long and expensive, and some legal commentators have suggested that the Convention should be incorporated into domestic law, so that the delay and high cost could be reduced. It has also been argued that the adoption of the Convention in both jurisdictions in Ireland might act as a reassurance of equality of rights. To date, however, politicians have been reluctant to face the possibility of an unpredictable and uncontrollable extension of legal support for human rights. The testing of the parameters of Bunreacht na hEireann, with the possibility of appeal to Strasbourg, seems to be regarded as sufficient safeguard.

### The Eighth Amendment

From 1981 until 1983 one of the most divisive debates in the Republic surrounded the eventually successful campaign for the Eighth Amendment to the Constitution to protect the life of the 'unborn'. Abortion seemed to be prohibited perfectly adequately by an 1861 Act. Moreover, the overwhelming majority of those campaigning against the Amendment were at pains to point out that they did *not* want to see abortion introduced; they were against the Eighth Amendment because they saw it as unnecessary and divisive. The campaign can be understood, however, only in terms of a fear that judicial interpretation, whether in Ireland itself or at the European Court of Human Rights, might change the existing law, and permit abortion 'by the back door'.

The Eighth Amendment was eventually passed in 1983. It illustrates well the difficulties presented by a written

Constitution which seeks to make detailed prohibitions and regulations – matters which might better be left to legislation. The 'X Case', as it became known, highlighted ambiguities in the Eighth Amendment. A court injunction was issued under the amendment in February 1992 restraining a young girl, pregnant as a result of rape, from leaving Ireland to seek an abortion. After numerous twists and turns, including some unexpected judicial rulings, it was necessary to have a triple referendum on various aspects of the abortion issue. Held in November 1992, it showed the public, like its politicians, to be somewhat equivocal. Two proposed amendments, relating to the right to travel (to have an abortion) and the right to information (about the availability of abortion in other countries) were passed; the third, on the more substantive issue of abortion itself, was defeated. The questions raised by the 'X Case' remained unresolved; while Irish people seem content to permit their fellow citizens to avail of abortion services in another jurisdiction, they are unwilling to permit abortions to be carried out in Ireland.

### Divorce and the Constitution

Another constitutional amendment campaign was fought in 1986, this time about the deletion of the Article in Bunreacht na hEireann which decreed that 'no law shall be enacted providing for the grant of a dissolution of marriage' (41.3.2). At the beginning, opinion polls showed a significant majority in favour of the change. However, the public debate became particularly enmeshed in the question of what it seemed might be the inadequate rights of a woman to a share of the family property after a divorce. The opinion polls began a slide which culminated in success for the 'no divorce' side. A case was also taken to the European Court of Human Rights by an Irish couple to test whether the Irish constitutional prohibition on divorce contravened their rights and those of their daughter, but it too was lost.

However, the divorce issue refused to go away. The anti-divorce view remained strong of course, but there were many for whom the availability of divorce was at the very top of what had begun to be called the 'liberal agenda' in Ireland. There were indeed people who were personally committed to the Catholic Church's view of life-long marriage, but for whom the question was nonetheless to do with personal liberty – about freedom of conscience, and about the need for Irish society to become more open and pluralistic.

After long and diligent preparation by the government, including legislation in advance to deal with the property rights aspect, in November 1995 the issue of divorce was again put to a referendum. The Irish people are not to be taken for granted, however. For despite the quite remarkable all-party support for the carefully worded proposition, only a slender majority favoured allowing divorce in Ireland.

## The effects of the situation in Northern Ireland

For some the implementation of the liberal agenda, as well as being necessary on its merits, is also important in order to convince Unionists in Northern Ireland that they have nothing to fear from their southern neighbours. However, the major effect of the initial outbreak of civil unrest in Northern Ireland in the 1960s was to bring the 'national question' back on to the political stage in the Republic. Bunreacht na hEireann claims the whole island of Ireland as being 'the national territory' (Article 2). It also asserts that although its practical effect is presently confined to the twenty-six counties, this is no way affects 'the right of the Parliament and Government established by this Constitution to exercise jurisdiction over the whole of [the national] territory' (Article 3).

For Unionists, Articles 2 and 3 have come to symbolise what they see as the hostile territorial ambitions of the Republic. In a case taken by a leading member of the Ulster Unionist Party in 1990 (*McGimpsey v. Ireland*), the Supreme Court said that Article 2 was a 'claim of legal right' on the whole island. Further, Article 3 was ruled to be a 'constitutional imperative'. The judgment does not specifically oblige the Republic's government to take any action on that score, however, and repeated formal recognitions of the status of Northern Ireland as part of the United Kingdom have been given. Nevertheless, it is likely that Articles 2 and 3 will be changed as part of any general settlement of the constitutional problems of Northern Ireland.

At an early stage of the present troubles in Northern Ireland, a referendum was held in order to refute, to at least some degree, Unionist assertions that the Republic was a sectarian state. Article 44.1.2 of Bunreacht na hEireann recognised 'the special position of the Holy Catholic Apostolic and Roman Church as the guardian of the faith professed by the great majority of the citizens'. Cross-party and wide social support ensured the easy passage of a referendum in 1972 calling for its deletion. The Article, it was argued, gave no rights or advantages to the Catholic Church, but it had negative connotations for Protestants and ought thus to be eliminated.

## Conclusions

Bunreacht na hEireann retains many of the features of British constitutional practice, to which the authors of Ireland's various Constitutions have looked for a model. It is, however, different in several important respects. The people are sovereign; the Head of State is elected; various Catholic sentiments are reflected in its working; vocationalism is the basis of the second chamber; and, most significant of all, it is written down. In many states the courts, by interpreting the constitution, play an increasingly forthright role in curbing governments and creating laws. Ireland, while retaining many British constitutional features, therefore, is becoming more like the United States, Germany, South Africa and elsewhere as regards judicial activism. The basis of the authority of judges derives from three sources: the written text; the increased intrusiveness of the state into the citizen's daily life; and broad consent in a popular culture that is cautious about the motives of politicians. In Ireland, the judiciary and jurists have found more scope for activism in the 1937 Constitution than they for long realised. The impact of legislation, especially the increasing EU-derived laws, has also alerted

Irish citizens to their constitutional rights. Finally, judges still command a high level of public respect for their impartiality and propriety.

Bunreacht na hEireann is, for all that, still bound by the ideological concerns, the political fears and the political aspirations of its authors. Half a century after it was written some of its provisions appear less well founded than de Valera, its principle progenitor, expected. A number of its novel features, such as the vocational second chamber, have developed quite differently than expected. Furthermore, attitudes today to such matters as the role of women and relations with Northern Ireland are in sharp contrast to those that shaped the original document. Nevertheless, the Constitution as amended, interpreted and informally augmented by politicians, civil servants and judges remains central to Irish politics today. As a working set of rules and principles, it has become the focus of debate about new social and political rights and obligations. Alterations to it are one important measure of the pace of social and political change.

## Notes

1 The European Court of Human Rights, based in Strasbourg, should not be confused with the European Court of Justice in Luxembourg, which is the European Union's main judicial body.
2 Only a Council of Europe member state's own constitutional provisions cannot be challenged.

## Further reading

B. Chubb, *Sourcebook of Irish Government*, Dublin: Institute of Public Administration, 1983.
B. Doolan, *Constitutional Law and Constitutional Rights in Ireland*, Dublin: Gill & Macmillan, 1984.
B. Farrell, *De Valera's Constitution and Ours*, Dublin: Gill & Macmillan, 1988.
A. Ward, *Constitutional Tradition: Government and Modern Ireland, 1782–1992*, Dublin: Irish Academic Press, 1994.

# 6

# Local government

Irish local government is less powerful and provides fewer services than in most other European countries. There is no recent tradition of local autonomy, and an *ultra vires* rule prevents local authorities from broadening their functions beyond those which central government permits to them. At the moment the list is dominated by housing, roads, water supply, sanitary services, development control and environmental protection. It is likely that this latter area will become more significant as public concern with the environment puts pressure on central government. Similarly for some authorities, libraries and swimming pools may be the focus of increased public demand. In 1996, the government accepted a list of minor administrative tasks, e.g., most grant applications in the area of housing, as functions which could be devolved to local government. On the other hand, some tasks, such as vehicle licensing, presently carried out by local government, may be removed – as was the provision of health services some years ago.

So the term 'local government' has encompassed a varying collection of tasks down through the years (including the upkeep of courthouses, the dipping of sheep against scabs, and the rehabilitation of travelling people). But whatever such changes there may have been from time to time, the local authorities themselves have proved fundamentally enduring, and they remain a vital part of Irish democracy. It is possible, if a consensus was reached between the main parties at national level, that local government may become significantly more powerful as a service provider by the turn of the century.

## The historical background

Local government in Ireland is based upon nineteenth-century British legislation that provided for single-tier urban and two-tier rural government. The services it provides are broadly similar to its British equivalent, but without responsibility for education, the police and many social services. Following their accounting practices, local government services can be described under the seven headings of: housing and building; road transportation and safety; water supply and sewerage; development incentives and controls; environmental protection; recreation and amenity; and, miscellaneous services. Housing (20 per cent), roads (35 per cent) and water and sewerage (11 per cent) account for the bulk of expenditure. A further function, education, is provided through the Vocational Education Committees, which have their own corporate status.

The chief innovations in local government since independence have involved the establishment of a national agency for local government appointments (1926); a concentration of administrative powers in the office of the City or County Manager (1940); and, the abolition of the domestic rating system (1978). The major Irish legislation is, in effect, a number of nineteenth-century British statutes, with a time lag, e.g., first came the 1888 (British) Local Government Acts, and only afterwards the 1898 (Irish) Local Government Acts.

The five major urban authorities, formally called 'county boroughs', cover the larger cities: Dublin, Cork, Limerick, Waterford and Galway. As well as the county borough called Dublin Corporation, the Dublin area has three county councils: Dún Laoghaire-Rathdown, Fingal and South Dublin. The rest of the country is divided into twenty-five county council areas, some of which have subordinate authorities within them – known as urban district councils (forty-nine) and town commissioners (twenty-six). Each local authority comprises two elements – the

Table 6.1 *Percentage of first preference votes in selected local, Dáil and European elections, 1979–1991*

| Party | Local 1979 | Euro 1984 | Local 1985 | Dáil 1987 | Dáil 1989 | Euro 1989 | Local 1991 |
|---|---|---|---|---|---|---|---|
| Fianna Fáil | 39 | 39 | 46 | 44 | 44 | 32 | 38 |
| Fine Gael | 35 | 32 | 30 | 27 | 29 | 22 | 27 |
| Labour | 12 | 8 | 8 | 6 | 10 | 10 | 11 |
| Others | 14 | 20 | 16 | 22 | 17 | 36 | 24 |

*Source:* Department of the Environment Reports.

elected members (councillors) and a Manager. County boroughs have between fifteen and fifty-two members; county councils range from twenty to forty-eight; and, the rest usually have nine members.

## Local elections

At the most recent major local government elections,[1] held in 1991, Fianna Fáil gained almost 41 per cent of the seats – a steep decline compared with their previous performance, in 1985. As in national contests, local elections use the STV system in multi-member constituencies. Local government elections are held infrequently, being regularly postponed for national political reasons – usually because the government party or parties fear heavy losses. Elections at a local level are, however, important: they influence local policies and services, and provide a further opportunity for democratic participation; those elected constitute the electoral college for most of the seats in the Seanad; and, local office holding is, as will be discussed below, a major route of entry into national politics. Some election statistics for the years 1979–1991 are provided in Tables 6.1 and 6.2.

For these reasons local elections are keenly contested, and a recurring theme is the financing of local government, especially the level of water and other service charges (on which see more below). More often than not, they produce a swing against the

Table 6.2 *Percentage of seats won in local elections, 1979-1991*

| Party | 1979 | 1985 | 1991 |
|-------|------|------|------|
| Fianna Fáil | 43 | 49 | 41 |
| Fine Gael | 39 | 32 | 31 |
| Labour | 10 | 7 | 10 |
| Others | 8 | 12 | 18 |

*Source:* Department of the Environment Reports

government of the day – though not always to the benefit of the main opposition party. On the whole, this has meant that Fianna Fáil is less well represented at local than at national level. Independents tend to do better, partly because the number of votes needed to be elected is quite low, and local concerns are more salient.

### The managerial system

The institution of the City or County Manager is the most distinctive and innovative feature of Irish local government. Broadly the Manager replaced the executive committees of the British system. He 'reports' his decisions to the council; its ability to overturn them is limited but somewhat controversial – as we shall see. The management system was intended mainly to bring about efficient and honest local administration. The period of civil turmoil leading up to 1922 had seen a decline in standards of administration and accounting. Cumann na nGaedheal governments acted quickly and resolutely to stamp out malpractice, and even suspended some local authorities altogether. Appointments procedures, auditing and other practices were reformed and public confidence in local government restored.

The management system was a response to public dissatisfaction with the role of the commissioners who had replaced suspended local authorities. It was first tried in the cities of Cork,

Dublin and Limerick, and by 1942 was in place throughout Ireland. The Managers themselves have become accepted as being above political suspicion, and the public image of local government has improved considerably, reflecting their key contribution to Irish life. They are also the only senior public servants in the Republic who account for their actions in public, on a monthly basis. However, like other top bureaucrats, their tenure is limited to a seven-year term.

Managers are selected by the Local Appointments Commission (LAC), which has been a major factor in establishing the reputation for honesty and diligence of local government officers. Women, however, fill only 3 per cent of all senior local government posts. As late as 1996, no woman had ever been a City or County Manager; and there were only two female county secretaries and one female finance officer. A report commissioned by the Dáil's Joint Committee on Women's Rights showed that, while women in the local government services were generally ambitious, local authorities varied widely in the gender balance among senior officers. While the LAC acts independently, other councils may soon wish to follow the example of Dublin Corporation's councillors, who in 1996 publicly outlined the specific qualities which they expected in their new City Manager. Addressing the gender imbalance may become a criterion.

In the 1960s Seán Lemass recognised that local authorities had an expanded role to play in national development. He talked of local authorities as 'development corporations', and most Managers have sought to fulfil this role, despite legal and financial restrictions. The Managers have offered leadership in policy formulation and direction generally. Much of the local development function has, however, been shared in recent years with other bodies such as state agencies, local community-based groupings, 'Partnership Companies', LEADER groups and others funded by the EU Structural Funds. The Devolution Commission suggested in 1996 that local authorities take a more central role in a new integrated system of local development. If this occurs, the Managers' involvement will be central though senior councillors will also be involved. Traditionally, the contribution of elected politicians has been to legitimise the leadership offered by their Manager, and to ease the execution of policy by intervening on behalf of aggrieved citizens. In future, they may take a more pro-active role but they will still experience electoral pressure to adopt a very localist perspective.

## The removal of domestic rates

Irish civil servants and ministers talk of local democracy, but in practice have held a tight rein on the local authorities. In the recent past this tendency was accentuated by economic and fiscal crises, obliging governments to seek to increase the amount of locally raised revenue. Moreover, the proportion of GNP accounted for by local spending had risen by the late 1970s to 17 per cent, compared to 10 per cent of a much smaller GNP in 1939. Local government finances have traditionally been drawn from state grants, from charges for services and, above all from 'domestic rates', a local property tax.

In 1977, the Fianna Fáil election manifesto promised to abolish rates on private homes – the central component of the party's election strategy. The promise was fulfilled after Fianna Fáil's landslide victory, by the Local Government (Financial Provisions) Act 1978. The Act meant that central government undertook to reimburse local authorities for all of the loss of rate income from private dwellings and certain other properties, including secondary schools and community halls. Rates on business properties remained, though they represented only a small proportion of the total locally generated income.

Crucially, the 1978 Act gave the Minister for the Environment a power of limitation with regard to local authority finance. Although local councils still set a theoretical 'rate', the minister is able to order a maximum on any increase – to prevent 'local authorities from increasing rates indiscriminately'. This of course has drastically curtailed the financial independence of local government. The loss of the rates as an independent local tax has had a marked effect. The most visible symbol of local autonomy, setting the rate level, was in effect removed. Instead the rate level has become an instrument of central government economic management and, as a consequence, been held well below inflation.

Between 1978 and 1981 local authorities adjusted to the new regime of high inflation and decreasing income by reducing the level of services provided, and by running down financial reserves – the impact varying according to the levels of rates in 1977, and to the reserves of the particular authority. However, there is no mechanism for rate 'equalisation', and some authorities, especially in areas of urban growth, enjoyed a degree of rate buoyancy from new developments. On the whole, however, the effect on local government was general cutbacks, restrictions and retrenchment. The system suffered a corresponding decrease in the morale of the staff, in its public image, and in its basic effectiveness.

## Service charges

The 1982 government circular on rates introduced a new element to local authority finance. While notifying a 15 per cent increase in permitted maximum rate levels, it also announced a shortfall in the level of grant. The government was going to put up only 92 per cent of the actual figures; the gap was to be made up by each authority levying charges for services provided. The minister promised to introduce the appropriate legislation 'at an early date'. This would, firstly, provide for a scale of fees for planning applications for building; and, secondly, give local authorities a general power to charge for local services. The idea of charges as a way of reducing local taxation had been mooted as far back as the 1960s, but its introduction in 1982 was unexpected.

The aims of central government in relation to fiscal and monetary policies plainly have little to do with individual local authority needs. Nevertheless, provoked by an unrelated fiscal crisis in the 1980s, central government has since sought to shift part of its burden to local government. Funding from the centre now falls short of local authority spending, so charges for local services are needed to make up the difference. Thus, it is argued, as well as making local authorities into tax gatherers, central government is also using them as a means of deflecting criticism from itself, of raising finance and of reducing public expenditure. Councils incur the odium of the public, but are unable to improve their income sufficiently without imposing more charges on the public. Water charges have been particularly unpopular and difficult to collect, and residents resent what they see simply as rates in a new guise. Indeed, service charges are politically so controversial that many local authorities have preferred to cut services rather than charge for them.

Governments have recently come to recognise the need to break the cycle of retrenchment in local authority services and increases in prices. The introduction of a general property tax has, however, been electorally unpopular; nor has it proved very productive in revenue terms; and its proceeds are not given directly to local government in any case.

It is worth taking note, finally, of some statistics on local government expenditure. Currently local authorities spend about 5.5 per cent of GNP. This consists of current spending (approximately 65 per cent of the total) and capital expenditure (roughly 35 per cent). Almost all of the capital spending is funded by central government grants; this covers major construction such as roads, water and sanitary service facilities and much of the public housing programme.

## Local politicians

After independence, the new government took a series of steps to assert central authority in areas of local government remuneration and recruitment. A central recruitment body the Local Appointments Commission, was a major departure from practice in Britian, where each local authority was responsible for recruiting its own staff. Thus, Irish local government officers do not depend on councillors for appointment or promotion. This gives the bureaucrats, especially the Manager, a significant degree of independence from the pressure of elected members on their councils.

The politician's role in local affairs is predominantly to offer to be an intermediary between constituents and the broad range of state bureaucracy. Local government is likely to be only one of his or her concerns. For the most part, Irish politicians are 'local politicians', however high they may climb in the elected hierarchy, for most TDs are also local councillors. Very few deputies, except ministers and their 'shadows', ever have to broaden their consideration of the purposes of local authorities beyond that of sources of individual benefits and electoral advantage. In practice, the current *modus operandi*, under which policy initiatives remain with the Manager, suits the politicians. Too close an association with controversial general policies would endanger their brokerage power base. At the same time most Managers can accommodate the needs of politicians for 'apparent' influence without seriously compromising general policy.

## Some controversial powers

The only major exceptions to the established understanding between politicians and the City or County Manager arise in relation to planning controls. Councillors in some authorities make regular use of their residual power to overturn a Manager's decision as it applies to a particular individual. This power is generally described with reference to its statutory basis in Section 4 of the County Management Act 1955. A Section 4 motion, if passed, permits a council to direct the Manager to act in a specific instance in a particular way. Typically, it allows planning permission to an individual where general criteria would indicate refusal. Often such cases concern the building of individual houses outside the general terms of the development plan for the area.

About half of all newly built private houses in Ireland are now 'one-off' homes, many built in spite of planning and other public considerations. In several counties this contravention of planning rules is regularly achieved by 'Section 4s'. Unlike other state benefits – like council houses and roads – planning permissions 'cost' councils nothing, and are in unlimited supply. Furthermore, once a council has established a pattern of such Section 4 permissions, it is difficult to stop granting them because refusal becomes politically costly.

The other major display of 'councillor power' comes with the adoption and adaptation of the local development plan. Each major council is the planning authority for its area, and as such is legally obliged to draw up a development plan showing the proposed pattern of land use. Thus the development plan divides the county or city into zones in which residential, agricultural, industrial or other activities will predominate. Planning applications are allowed or refused with reference to the development plan. Clearly the commercial value of land is markedly influenced by the category into which it is zoned. The pressure on politicians to assert their legal rights can be very great, and developers often offer to provide extra amenities, such as sports facilities and parks, if land is made available for residential or industrial use.

In September 1995 serious allegations of corruption in the planning process led to the establishment of a formal state investigation. The great majority of elected members and officials have, of course, never been involved in impropriety. Rumours of a corrupt few are nevertheless damaging to the reputation of all. Previous Garda inquiries have got nowhere, because the law in the area of corruption is completely out of date. It is likely that new legislation will soon be introduced to make the prevention of corruption in local government easier.

Controversial in some local authorities has been the approval of the annual budget, with some councillors refusing to adopt the Managers' estimates. The issue, in almost all cases, has been the inclusion of new service charges to which the councillors object. This was particularly disputatious in the Dublin area councils. The Minister for the Environment threatened to remove such authorities from office, and to appoint commissioners in their place. On each occasion, however, as with Fingal, South Dublin and Dún Laoghaire/Rathdown in February 1994, the councils eventually adopted the estimates after a period of protest and brinkmanship. The real conflict, needless to say, had been between the council and central government rather than with the Manager.

## Pressure groups

The position that the Manager holds in relation to the elected representatives of his area is a by-product of political competition. There are few rewards for the politician in competing with the Manager for control over most areas of policy. Nor does the public put much pressure on councillors to fight on a broad policy front. Indeed, pressure group activity involving local government has until recently been very limited, particularly outside Dublin. The major national pressure groups, especially those representing farming and business, are organised at a sub-national level but they rarely operate through county or city councillors. On local government issues, the major interest groups will generally communicate with the appropriate officials directly, or in counties especially, through the Manager. Cultural, social and sporting groups rarely exert pressure on local government at the level of broad policy. There is a virtual consensus in Ireland on housing and welfare provision, which is only strained significantly for local authorities in relation to the settlement of travelling people, and the provision of halting sites for those who 'remain on the road'.

The activity of pressure groups in Irish local government, then, is largely confined to detailed and specific provisions – such as road improvements or refuse collection. On these issues, residents' associations or *ad hoc* groups may solicit the support of local politicians, and such pressure sometimes does cause a particular decision to be reviewed. The exception to this particularistic, low-key pressure group activity concerns major planning applications, such as the siting of gas or oil storage facilities, or such nationally organised campaigns as there are against service charges. In both cases the issues involved ultimately transcend the local arena, and the crucial decisions are made at the national level.

Most councillors only become involved when the pressure group's request is local, specific, achievable in the short term, and open to favourable publicity. Further, councillors may wish to avoid association with issues that too obviously divide the local electorate. In case of a councillor coming under local pressure, he or she might be pleased that the Manager will publicly accept responsibility for unpopular decisions. Not surprisingly, pressure group activity is greatest in urban areas. For example, people in new housing developments quickly form residents' associations. Local politicians tend to become involved in such groups at an early stage, in order to prevent them from becoming alternative routes for complaint.

In some urban areas, local political activists have been using residents' associations to challenge the hegemony of the established political parties. Again councillors, TDs and their supporters see this development as a challenge, and respond by seeking to enhance their own ability to respond to 'client groups'. Thus a number of advice centres associated with particular parties or politicians have been opened in several urban areas in Dublin and elsewhere. Some of these offices are well equipped – with word processors, telephone answering machines, photocopiers and so on. Their aim, however, is to provide the traditional politician's services more efficiently.

### The reform of local government

In March 1991 an expert committee, asked by the government to look into the structures and functions (though not the funding) of local government, recommended fairly radical reforms. Like various reports before it, however, the Barrington Report (as it became known) was followed by minimal changes. Legislation in 1992 provided for a slight relaxation of the *ultra vires* rule, which empowered councils to take actions not formerly permitted which might be 'in the interests of the local community'. It did not, however, include a prohibition on the 'dual mandate' that Barrington had proposed. This would have prevented TDs, Senators and MEPs from also being councillors.

Such a change, which would have a marked impact on electoral politics, is still widely canvassed.

Another possible reform might be the strengthening of the institution of Lord Mayor, or Council Chairman. Currently these posts are largely ceremonial, and are filled annually by election within the council. A former Lord Mayor of Dublin has suggested a directly elected mayor standing on a city-wide basis – as in some US cities. Such a democratically responsible official could more easily resist the pressures of local councillors; the new mayor or chairperson would complement the leadership role of the Manager and help in the formulation and accomplishment of difficult policies. The time may now be right for a change in the respective roles of bureaucrat and politician in Irish local government.

Finally, the Constitution Review Group recommended that a form of 'recognition in principle of local government' should be inserted in the Constitution. Such a reform would bring Ireland into line with most other EU states. It would also be in accordance with the European Charter of Local Self Government of the Council of Europe, which the government said in 1996 that it was considering adopting.

### Regions

The attitude of central government to local government is heavily influenced by the belief that Ireland already has too many elected local authorities and members. Critics of this view point to the lack of comparative international evidence, and argue that had Ireland gone through the radical overhaul of local government common in other European countries in recent decades, there would probably be more rather than less local government. However, officials of the Department of the Environment seem firmly convinced of the need reduce the number of councils and councillors.

Eight regional authorities were nevertheless established in 1994, roughly along the lines suggested in the Barrington Report. They are statutory bodies comprising local elected representatives, selected by constituent local authorities. In total, the regional authorities have 220 members. Their main tasks are to promote the coordination of public services in their regions, and to review and advise on the implementation of EU Structural and Cohesion Fund Programmes. Provision has been made for an operational committee to advise and assist each authority. This committee includes the constituent City or County Managers and the chief executives of various public bodies in the region.

The European Commission has long advocated powerful regional structures in all member states, as a means of devolving power over the spending of EU money to local communities. Irish ministers have resisted such moves because the central government, by contrast, wishes to retain financial control of all EU funds. Ironically, a reversal of policy may now be forced on Ireland by its own economic success. Under established criteria, member states need to have 80 per cent or less of the EU average income per head to qualify for maximum levels of EU support; but treated as a single region, Ireland may soon no longer qualify. To avoid losing substantial EU receipts, therefore, Ireland may have to establish a stronger regional structure. In this way the poorer parts of the state would continue to benefit from EU structural and cohesion funding.

## Conclusions

Local government in Ireland, as an independent, adequately resourced and innovative part of the nation's life, has been on the decline since the 1970s. The keys to its reduced role are the lack of sufficient truly local revenue, the neglect of its long-term future by central government, and some public indifference to local democracy. In partial recognition of the truth of all this, in July 1995 the government set up a Devolution Commission to examine how 'significant additional functions' could be devolved to local authorities.

The Commission worked closely with a cabinet committee chaired by the Taoiseach. This initiative resonated clearly with previous inquiries: in particular, the Commission cited the need for increased local accountability, and for the principle of subsidiarity, as the starting points on any review. In August 1996, the government accepted a recommendation of the Commission that a new local government system should have three tiers: regional, with a mainly coordinating function; county, with county councils as the primary unit of local government with a broader remit; and sub-county, with elected local authorities in towns. The government also decided that an integrated local government and local development system would come into operation on 1 January 2000, on completion of the current round of spending under the EU Community Support Framework for Ireland. In the interim, local authorities will be encouraged to develop a more structured relationship with the local development bodies active in their area.

A series of other government-commissioned reports, published in June 1996, covered possible funding mechanisms and local government boundaries. The consultants were conservative in their recommendations on changing the current local government map, but did favour a local property tax or a local income tax. Receiving the reports, the Minister for the Environment asked for an all-party committee to try to reach some consensus on the financing of local government. The opposition parties reacted cautiously. It seems that much more political commitment would need to be shown if these reports are to have more impact than their predecessors.

### Note

1 Elections were held for the smaller urban district councils in 1994.

### Further reading

N. Collins, *Local Government Managers at Work*, Dublin: Institute of Public Administration, 1987.

M. Coughlan and D. deBuitleir, *Local Government Finance in Ireland*, Dublin: Institute of Public Administration, 1996.

D. Roche, *Local Government in Ireland*, Dublin: Institute of Public Administration, 1982.

# 7

# Northern Ireland

Northern Ireland became a separate political entity in 1921, being one of the two Irish states which the 1920 Government of Ireland Act was intended to create. 'Northern Ireland', was to consist of the six north eastern counties, and 'Southern Ireland', the rest of the island. Because of the continuing military turmoil, the Home Rule plan came into effect only in Northern Ireland, which also remained a part of the United Kingdom. The broad intention of the Ulster Unionist Party at its formation was to have the whole nine counties of the ancient Province of Ulster remain in Union with Britain. Had this come to pass, however, Northern Ireland would have contained a precariously small majority of voters in favour of the Union. The actual boundary was, therefore, dictated by a need to balance maximisation of Northern Ireland's land area with ensuring a permanent and secure unionist majority. With this guarantee of continuous power, the Ulster Unionists took over the reins and enjoyed fifty years of uninterrupted one-party rule – that is, until the prorogation (or suspension) of the Northern Ireland parliament in 1972.

Political and religious antagonisms in Northern Ireland have flared into civil disorder as well as armed action periodically since the IRA mounted its first offensive against the new regime in the early 1920s. On the whole, however, Unionist governments managed to repress dissent and keep a generally firm grip on affairs until the late 1960s. To use a mechanical analogy,

Northern Ireland was maintained in a state of unstable equilibrium. This equilibrium was occasionally disturbed, but was only finally upset when politics moved on to the streets in 1968. The current 'troubles' were precipitated initially by the failure of the liberal wing of the Unionist Party to persuade traditionalist colleagues that it was necessary to accede to at least some of the demands of the burgeoning civil rights movement. These demands arose out of a perception – borne out to be correct by research undertaken since then – of determined discrimination against Catholics down through the years, in almost all areas of social and economic life.[1] A variety of reforms were called for: a fairer system for the allocation of public housing; the extension of the local government franchise from householders only to all adults, together with the elimination of multiple voting rights based on ownership of property (jointly encapsulated in the slogan 'one-man-one-vote'); an end to the gerrymandering – or distortion – of constituency boundaries (which ensured continuing Unionist domination in key local government areas); and legislation to ensure fair and equal employment opportunities for all.

The civil rights movement began from a wide political base, with representation from all parts of the political spectrum; and its demands were principally for rights which the citizens of the rest of the UK already enjoyed. Despite that, the Northern Ireland government claimed that 'civil rights' was simply a new cover for nationalist agitation – and that the Union with Britain was thus threatened.[2] Ironically, although the Protestant working class suffered many of the same disadvantages as did Catholics, most ordinary Protestants accepted the government's interpretation of the protests as a republican plot. The mainly Protestant security forces were thus deployed to maintain order; marches and meetings were broken up; and the police were sometimes seen to be cooperating with Protestant counter-protesters. During 1969 a number of major stand-offs between protestors and the Royal Ulster Constabulary (RUC) occurred simultaneously across Northern Ireland, which stretched the police to breaking point.

The British government was finally forced to intervene, and troops were put on to the streets in large numbers in an effort to restore order.

In the period that followed, London continued to put pressure for reform on the Unionist government, and several important concessions were made to the civil rights demands. A step too far for the Unionists, however, was a proposal that all responsibility for security be taken over by London. Their defiance brought about the suspension of Northern Ireland's parliament and government in March 1972. Since then, apart from a short interregnum in 1974, direct rule from London has been carried on under a UK cabinet minister, the Secretary of State for Northern Ireland.

In the meantime the almost entirely peaceful protests of the civil rights movement had been overtaken by a major surge of violence initiated principally by the IRA. Acting in Britain as well as Northern Ireland, the IRA's campaign of 'armed struggle' has consisted of two main strands: firstly, the bombing of what it describes as 'economic targets' – restoration or replacement of which would be a significant charge on the British government; secondly, the killing, by a variety of means, of serving and former soldiers and policemen. However, there has sometimes been a calculated sectarian element in IRA activity (including the killing of uninvolved Protestants, using cover names such as the 'Catholic Action Force'). Predominantly as a response to the IRA's campaign, two paramilitary organisations loyal to the union with Britain, the Ulster Volunteer Force (UVF) and the Ulster Defence Association (UDA), have engaged in a counter-campaign which has consisted mainly of the random assassination of Catholics. By 1996 the violence in Northern Ireland had claimed more than 3,000 lives – military, paramilitary and civilian – and over 30,000 injuries.

### Religion and political divisions

Discussion of the politics of Northern Ireland is often expressed in religious terms, which seem anachronistic to the outsider. It is useful, therefore, before going on to describe Northern Ireland's institutions, to discuss briefly the nature of the division.

The roots of the problem in Northern Ireland can be traced to the differential success of colonial policy in Ireland. As was discussed in Chapter 3, plantation was the means by which British rule was established. An attempt was made to uproot one group of people, the native Catholics, and replace them with English and Scottish Protestants whose loyalty was assured. The greater success of the policy in the northeast set the province of Ulster apart. The plantation began in earnest in 1607 and was largely over by 1641, but it established the current pattern of social, religious, political and economic division. It is broadly true that there are still two camps, and the rallying calls of the main political forces thus tend to appeal to each community separately.

The Protestant majority in Northern Ireland belongs to a number of denominations, the two largest being the Presbyterian Church in Ireland (which has some Scottish associations) and the Church of Ireland (the Irish wing of the Anglican/Episcopalian family). For many fundamentalist Protestants, Northern Ireland is the last bastion of the true tradition of the Reformation. It stands alone in battle against secularism, communism and, above all, Popery – as Roman Catholicism is pejoratively described.[3] For loyalists – the name generally used to describe the most militant advocates of the maintenance of the Union – the link with the British Crown is also a guarantee of Protestant hegemony, which could not, of course, be sustained in an overwhelmingly Catholic united Irish state. The Orange Order, a religious-cum-political organisation to which many Unionist politicians belong, epitomises these values. Indeed, if Britain were to weaken its commitment to Northern Ireland, many loyalists would actually demand independence rather than accept an all-Ireland settlement.

The great bulk of unionists, on the other hand, wish to remain British for economic and sentimental rather than religious reasons. They want the British government's large financial subvention, which ensures that living standards have been generally higher in Northern Ireland than in the Republic, to be maintained. They also wish to retain their links to the wider British community, with its cultural traditions, its liberal democratic institutions, the Queen, the Union flag and the Commonwealth. Moreover, a significant number of such unionist-minded people have come to consider the fifty years of 'Home Rule' in Northern Ireland a mistake. The argument is that this was bound to exacerbate community divisions by making politics almost entirely about Partition. They now favour fully 'reintegrating' Northern Ireland into the UK – so that it might be governed 'like Yorkshire', with no more than low-level local government institutions based in Northern Ireland itself.

The Catholic community forms just over 40 per cent of the population of Northern Ireland. It is, like its Protestant counterpart, divided by class and other social distinctions; for while Catholics suffer a disproportionate share of disadvantage, most are neither marginalised nor deprived, and the Catholic middle class has grown considerably in the last thirty years. In religious terms Catholicism also has its fundamentalists, and it is possible to detect a progressive–conservative divide, especially since the Second Vatican Council began to erode old doctrinal certainties. However, this has had no discernible effect on the politics of Northern Ireland. In political terms, while there is a traditional and enduring link between being a Catholic and being a nationalist, opinion polls indicate that significant numbers of Catholics are content for the Union with Britain to remain. What really unites Catholics, of all political complexions, is mistrust of Unionism – based on being at the hard end of fifty years of devolved government in Northern Ireland.

Day-to-day, each community is well nigh self-sufficient in social and cultural terms, and contact with 'the other side' – except in a workplace setting – is often perfunctory. Significantly, the great majority of Catholic children attend schools run under the auspices of the Roman Catholic Church, whose ethos is clearly denominational and often Irish in cultural outlook. Until recently, the cost to the Catholic community of such separate educational provision was that it had itself to raise a proportion of the capital costs involved. However, the UK government now meets in full both running costs and capital investment.

State schools are, for all practical purposes, Protestant schools; local Protestant clergy are entitled to be represented on their Boards of Governors; and they reflect, for the most part, a self-consciously British outlook. Barriers between the two school systems have been broken down to a limited extent by government-funded initiatives like the Education for Mutual Understanding and Cultural Heritage programmes. The UK government has also provided special funding for the development of religiously integrated education and, although still few in number, there are now integrated schools in all the main centres of population.

Since the Unionists saw as a central task the defence of Protestant interests, it was the clear strategy of government and local councils after 1922 to keep Catholics in an inferior economic position; in particular, it was necessary to prevent them from gaining a foothold in positions of political or administrative influence. As the then Prime Minister, Sir James Craig, told the Northern Ireland House of Commons in 1934: 'all I boast is that we are a Protestant Parliament and a Protestant State.'[4]

Unemployment in Northern Ireland has always run at higher levels than in the rest of the UK, and has been consistently at its worst in places where Catholics form a larger than average proportion of the population. For example, a historically lower level of industrial development left much of the west of Northern Ireland, where Catholics are in the majority, relatively deprived of job opportunities, in all sectors of the labour market. Although there is little evidence to support the contention that standard government economic development schemes were administered so as to ensure greater employment in Protestant areas, it is clear that the decision in the 1960s to site a new city (Craigavon) in the southeast, rather than develop the existing City of Derry/Londonderry, was motivated by fear that more Catholics than Protestants would have benefited from the latter.

The overall figures certainly support the claim of serious Catholic disadvantage. For example, in 1971 Catholic unemployment was 13.9 per cent while the Protestant figure was 5.6 per cent. Catholics were also more likely to be found in occupations which experience the highest rates of seasonal and long-term unemployment. Despite the British government's Fair Employment Act of 1976, and the major amendments made to it by the 1989 Act of the same name – which now provide Northern Ireland with the most forceful anti-discrimination legislation in Europe – the situation has not changed substantially since then. Catholics are still more than twice as likely to be unemployed as Protestants (in 1993 the Catholic figure was 23.1 per cent, and that for Protestants was 11.1 per cent); while Catholic representation in the civil and public services generally is now proportionately 'correct', they are still underrepresented at the most senior levels; and the same is true as regards higher management positions in the private sector. Instead, the Catholic middle classes are found disproportionately in the liberal professions such as the law and medicine, where entry is largely determined by educational achievement. As to why there has been so little change in the situation in the last twenty years, the much higher 1993 unemployment figures suggest that a major part of the explanation must lie in economic decline. Eliminating the imbalance not only requires many more new jobs but also a turnover of personnel in existing jobs – which does not happen when opportunities for mobility in the labour market are scarce.

The most obvious physical manifestation of community division in Northern Ireland is segregated public housing. For reasons of electoral advantage and social control, council houses were allocated on sectarian lines for many years. Indeed, if Northern Ireland then had the worst housing conditions in the UK, it was not entirely due to lack of resources. Londonderry Corporation actually refused to build any houses at all in the mid-1960s, because while the available land was in Unionist/Protestant electoral wards, the most likely tenants would have been Catholics. One of the civil rights demands which was responded to relatively quickly was the removal of housing functions from local authorities. These were assumed by an independent Housing Executive. Since the outbreak of the present 'troubles', the housing stock has undergone remarkable improvement. That said, the segregation of working-class housing on sectarian lines has actually increased during the last twenty-five years, as members of each community have sought safety in numbers. On the other hand, with the major exception of Derry, middle-class housing has generally remained 'integrated'.

## Parties and elections in Northern Ireland

Since 1922, the position of Northern Ireland within the UK – 'the constitutional issue' – has dominated local politics, but the 'sides' are internally divided. Dealing first with parties in favour of the Union with Britain, the Ulster Unionists (UUP) are not only the strongest party, but also the oldest. As already noted, the UUP held power in Northern Ireland continuously from 1921 until 1972. The Democratic Unionist Party (DUP) is more populist in approach, and was formed in 1971 by people who felt that the UUP was insufficiently resolute in defending the Union. Although these two parties cooperate from time to time, relationships have often been strained because of the very different styles of their respective leaderships. The Ulster Popular Unionist Party was the creature of a disaffected UUP MP, and itself expired soon after his death in 1995. The United Kingdom Unionists (UKU) was formed by his successor as MP for North Down; it seeks the full 'reintegration' of Northern Ireland with the rest of the UK. The Progressive Unionist Party (PUP) and the Ulster Democratic Party (UDP) have received much attention since the 1994 ceasefires (see below); they have their roots in the UVF and UDA respectively. The PUP and UDP are generally leftist in approach, having come to regard the two main Unionist parties as inherently unable to look after the interests of working-class Protestants.

'In the middle', together with some smaller groupings, is the Alliance Party. It was formed in 1970 with the intention of bringing Protestants and Catholics together to reach an agreed

Table 7.1 *Results in Northern Ireland of the 1992 Westminster election*

| Party name | No of votes | % vote | Change from 1987 | Candidates | Seats won | % seats |
|---|---|---|---|---|---|---|
| Ulster Unionist Party (UUP) | 271,049 | 34.5 | −3.3 | 13 | 9 | 52.9 |
| Social Democratic and Labour Party (SDLP) | 184,445 | 23.5 | +2.4 | 13 | 4 | 23.5 |
| Democratic Unionist Party (DUP) | 103,039 | 13.1 | +1.4 | 7 | 3 | 17.7 |
| Sinn Féin (SF) | 78,291 | 10.0 | −1.4 | 14 | | |
| Alliance Party | 68,665 | 8.7 | −1.3 | 16 | | |
| Conservative Party | 44,608 | 5.7 | +5.7 | 11 | | |
| Ulster Popular Unionists | 19,305 | 2.5 | 0 | 1 | 1 | 5.9 |
| Others | 15,691 | 2.1 | −3.3 | 25 | | |

*Source:* Based on report of results in *Irish Political Studies*, Vol. 8, 1993, p. 186.

settlement of the Northern Ireland problem, preferably within the Union. It is worthy of mention in passing that the political left has usually been in the middle also on the constitutional issue, but has enjoyed even less success than the labour tradition south of the border since Partition. In the 1996 Peace Forum elections (see below) the four declaredly left-wing groupings together gained only 1.5 per cent of the vote.

Also set up in 1970, after the effective demise of the old Nationalist Party, was the Social Democratic and Labour Party (SDLP). It is the largest nationalist party and, unlike its main rival for nationalist votes, has always been committed to peaceful democratic methods. Sinn Féin, which is closely associated with the IRA, has a much longer history and is more resolutely nationalist than the SDLP. Until recently, it endorsed the use of force in the pursuit of a united all-Ireland state. After the IRA ceasefire of August 1994, however, it began to distance itself, albeit somewhat tentatively, from the 'armed struggle'.

The UK general election of 1992 (see Table 7.1) illustrates the pattern of most recent contests – despite being slightly confused

Table 7.2 *Results in the 1996 elections to the Northern Ireland Peace Forum*

| Party name | No of votes | % vote |
|---|---|---|
| Ulster Unionist Party (UUP) | 181,829 | 24.2 |
| Social Democratic and Labour Party (SDLP) | 160,786 | 21.4 |
| Democratic Unionist Party (DUP) | 141,413 | 18.8 |
| Sinn Féin (SF) | 116,377 | 15.5 |
| Alliance Party | 49,176 | 6.5 |
| United Kingdom Unionists (UKU) | 27,774 | 3.7 |
| Progessive Unionist Party (PUP) | 26,082 | 3.5 |
| Ulster Democratic Party (UDP) | 16,715 | 2.2 |
| Conservative Party | 3,595 | 0.5 |
| Others | 27,595 | 3.8 |

*Source:* Based on local newspaper reports of results.

by the intervention of recently formed local branches of the British Conservative Party. A more up-to-date measure of electoral opinion is provided by the 1996 election (see Table 7.2) to choose members of the Northern Ireland Peace Forum – from among whom were selected the negotiating teams for the associated multi-party peace talks (see below). The main gainers were the DUP and Sinn Féin, and the main losers the UUP, Conservatives and Alliance. That there was virtually no crossing of the great divide is demonstrated by the fact that in percentage terms the total unionist vote remained firmly in the mid-fifties, while that of the nationalists stayed equally firmly in the mid-thirties.

### The Northern Ireland economy

Northern Ireland has been described as a caricature of a 'dependent economy': dependent on external funding, external ideas and external initiatives.[5] Dependence on British government aid is as characteristic of many Northern Ireland companies as it is of the economy as a whole; and the public sector accounts for roughly 35 per cent of those in employment. This reliance on public funding led Rowthorn to describe Northern Ireland as:

> a vast workhouse, in which most of the inmates are engaged in servicing or controlling each other . . . [It] imports a great deal from the outside world whilst providing few exports in return; moreover, as in the case of a workhouse or prison, the gap between imports and exports is financed out of taxes levied on the external population.[6]

The dependency thesis relies, of course, on viewing Northern Ireland as having a separate economy, rather than it being part of the wider UK economy – which plainly includes other areas in receipt of subvention from the centre. Be that as it may, it is the case that public expenditure *per capita* in Northern Ireland is about 30 per cent higher than the UK *average.*

### Industry

Northern Ireland began by being the most industrialised part of Ireland, but the seeds of a long-term decline in its staple industries – linen, shipbuilding and general engineering – had already been sown. By the late 1950s the economy was in serious difficulties and, like its counterpart in Dublin, the Northern Ireland government began to look abroad for investors. The particular success in this regard was man-made fibres; six major multinationals were persuaded to build huge plants which eventually employed many thousands of workers. But this was a short-lived phenomenon, and the industry collapsed in the early 1980s in face of cheaper supplies from low-wage, newly industrialising countries. International competition, together with various economic shocks, also had their effects on other sectors: woven textiles, clothing, tyre manufacture and tobacco products.

New 'high-tech' ventures have so far made only a minor contribution to employment, and the encouragement of local small enterprise has been effective merely at the margins. The result of all this is that, despite starting from very different positions three-quarters of a century ago, Northern Ireland and the

Republic now stand at close to the same point on a range of economic indicators.[7] Most remarkable is that while almost half the Northern Ireland workforce in the 1920s was engaged in industrial occupations, the figure today is below 25 per cent – almost exactly the same as south of the border.

As in the Republic, agriculture and food production remain the largest industries. In terms of wealth creation, they are also among the best performing sectors, with an annual gross output of £1,300 million. Over 60 per cent of what is produced is exported and some 20 per cent of Northern Ireland's workforce is engaged, directly or indirectly, in agriculture. An increasing proportion of the rural labour force is not, however, occupied full-time in agricultural production; farm-household incomes often depend to a significant extent on non-agricultural employment. UK and EU agricultural policies are likely to accentuate these trends. Moreover, the impact of change in the rural economy is greatest on the Catholic community which, because of the enduring effects of the plantation, generally owns the poorer land.

In broader terms, a lack of jobs remains the greatest scourge: the unemployment rate in the mid-1990s was running at between 13 and 14 per cent, as compared with around 7 per cent in Great Britain; some areas – West Belfast, Cookstown, parts of Derry and Strabane – reported male unemployment rates of more than 50 per cent; over half of those unemployed had been so for over a year (which compares with 35-40 per cent in the UK as a whole); and, as noted above, Catholics are still twice as likely to be out of work as Protestants.

Although somewhat later than in the rest of the UK, Northern Ireland has felt the rigours of Conservative economic policy: in particular, privatisation and competitive tendering for services formerly provided from within the public sector. The two major engineering operations remaining in Belfast – the Harland and Wolff shipyard and the Shorts' aircraft and armaments plants – were in public ownership for many years, but have now been privatised. So too have Northern Ireland Electricity and Belfast International Airport. Water supply and public transport will soon be candidates for the same treatment. Because of its high unemployment, to which these policies have added, and its greatly weakened manufacturing base, then, the Northern Ireland economy will continue to be dependent upon support from central government for some time to come.

## The institutions of government in Northern Ireland

As a result of the Government of Ireland Act 1920, a wide range of responsibilities – including education, health, personal social services, home affairs (including law and order), housing, planning and economic development – were devolved to the regional parliament and government in Belfast. Responsibility for certain other matters, such as foreign affairs, defence, taxation, government publications and the postal service, were reserved to the sovereign parliament in London, and continued to be administered in Northern Ireland by UK civil servants. However, a separate civil service – the Northern Ireland Civil Service (NICS) – was set up to administer the devolved functions. This structure survived until 1972, when the Northern Ireland parliament was prorogued; the NICS has remained in place, but the Secretary of State and a number of junior ministers in the Northern Ireland Office (NIO) now direct the work of Northern Ireland departments. As well as this quasi-supervisory role, the NIO is itself responsible for the contentious area of law and order, and for what is described as 'political development' – the search for a long term solution to the Northern Ireland problem.

The machinery of government and the delivery of public services have always been organised on a regional, sub-regional and local basis, and 'direct rule' has not altered this. There are presently six Northern Ireland government departments, the work of which includes coordinating the activities of sub-regional and local bodies. For example, housing policy, planning and other local services in general are the responsibility of the Department of Environment for Northern Ireland; but public housing is managed on its behalf by the Housing Executive. Similarly, the Department of Education is responsible not only for educational policy but also for oversight of the geographically based Education and Library Boards.

The principal role of the Department of Economic Development (DED) is to strengthen the economy through the generation of trade and industry, and it is assisted in this by two independently managed state bodies: the Local Enterprise Development Unit; and the Industrial Development Board, which has the particular task of attracting foreign investment. DED's other responsiblities include labour force matters such as industrial relations and industrial training; the registration of companies; consumer protection; health and safety at work; and equality of opportunity, especially in employment. The Department of Health and Social Services takes overall responsibility for all health, personal social services and social security matters, and has oversight of the sub-regional Health and Social Services Boards. The 'Treasury' role and the central management of the civil service are undertaken by the Department of Finance and Personnel.

Legislation at Westminster affecting Northern Ireland can be enacted in three ways. Firstly, Bills passed by parliament can be declared to have effect throughout the United Kingdom – in other words, to apply in Northern Ireland as well as England, Scotland and Wales. Secondly, important Bills which affect Northern Ireland alone may be dealt with using the full procedures of both Houses. This is, however, a fairly rare event. It is more usual to legislate on Northern Ireland matters using a third method: Orders in Council. Since debate is very restricted, and it is not possible for amendments to be proposed to such an Order, the process is the subject of frequent complaint by Members from Northern Ireland and their parliamentary allies. Partly in response to this pressure, in 1994 the government agreed to the setting up of a Northern Ireland Select Committee, intended to provide an additional forum for discussion of Northern Ireland issues.

A further institution was added to existing structures following the Anglo-Irish Agreement of 1985. It established an Intergovernmental Conference – a mechanism by which the government of the Republic is entitled to put forward its views on a range of matters affecting Northern Ireland. The Conference, which has a secretariat in Belfast staffed by both UK and Irish civil servants, meets regularly, and is chaired jointly by the Secretary of State for Northern Ireland and the Minister for Foreign Affairs from Dublin. Dominating the Conference's agenda until the early 1990s were three particular issues: the extradition of terrorist suspects from one jurisdiction to another; increasing the confidence of nationalists in the administration of justice in Northern Ireland; and addressing the disadvantage which Catholics suffer in the labour market. Since the Downing Street Declaration of December 1993, however, virtually all the Conference's attention has been diverted to the 'peace process' (on which see more below).

## Local government

As part of the process of removing contentious matters from the local council arena, the Local Government (Northern Ireland) Act, 1972, provided for the creation of twenty-six local authorities with responsibilities for relatively few executive functions. These include certain regulatory services, such as cinema and dance-hall licencing, building regulations and health inspection. Councils also provide a limited range of direct services to the public: street cleaning; refuse collection and disposal; burial grounds and crematoria; public baths; recreation facilities; and tourist amenities. Added to these recently has been the freedom to engage in certain local industrial development activities.

Refuse collection and disposal, and leisure and community services represent the only major items of expenditure by local authorities in Northern Ireland. As a consequence, local government is responsible for less than 3 per cent of total public expenditure. In addition to these executive responsibilities, local authorities have representative and consultative functions. Local authorities are entitled to representation on certain public agencies, advisory councils and the area boards, although – as in the rest of the UK – the government has reduced such representation in recent years and replaced nominees of councils by business people. Local councils are also consulted about matters for which they have no executive responsibility, such as proposed housing schemes, planning applications and road developments within their area.

Elections to the twenty-six local authorities are held every four years. The 1993 contest, which was an almost perfect re-run of that in 1989, left eighteen councils in the control of parties in favour of the Union with Britain. The UUP took 29 per cent of the total vote, the SDLP 22 per cent, the DUP 17 per cent, Sinn Féin 12 per cent, Alliance 8 per cent and 'others' 12 per cent. The district councils are the only forums in which locally elected politicians confront each other on a regular basis; so despite the councils' limited powers they are at the centre of frequent controversy. Debates on issues outside their strict remit are a regular feature, and it is here that much of Northern Ireland's day-to-day political drama is played out.

Against a background of contentious developments in Anglo-Irish relations (see below), the presence in significant numbers of Sinn Féin councillors, open supporters of the IRA, provoked much disruption of council business by Unionist members in the late 1980s and early 1990s. On the other hand, some non-unionist (generally SDLP) controlled councils have adopted a policy of 'power-sharing', which usually takes the form of a rotation of senior offices, such as mayor/council leader and committee chairs. This has had the effect of improving inter-party relations in some areas, and avoiding the bitterness which characterises the conduct of business on other councils. However, despite the more constructive approach of some councillors, local government will continue to be a focus for discontent until a wider political solution is arrived at which commands sufficient consent in both communities.[8]

## Northern Ireland and the European Union

Attitudes to the EU in Northern Ireland are ambivalent. Many Protestants and Unionists are suspicious of what they perceive to be the Catholic ethos of the EU, the implicit dilution of UK sovereignty, and the opportunity it has provided for the Republic to gain economic and political advantage. However, the benefits of the agricultural and regional policies are fully acknowledged. Northern Ireland has not done as well financially out of the EU as the Republic, but is still a considerable beneficiary, especially as regards development of the greater Belfast area. From a nationalist point of view, on the other hand, the evolution of the EU has decreased the significance of the Irish border, particularly since the elimination of customs controls following the completion of the internal market in 1992. This also makes it harder for Unionists to deny the mutual interests of the two parts of the island relative to Britain – all the more so since both Northern Ireland and the Republic are in the regional category which attracts the greatest assistance for economic development from Europe.

### Towards the settlement of an ancient quarrel?

Although a settlement in Northern Ireland seems as far away as ever, it is arguable that huge strides have been taken so far as the general understanding of the problem is concerned since the early 1980s. The first major move along the road was taken in the Republic, when the 'New Ireland Forum' met in Dublin in 1983. The Forum was composed of representatives of almost all political parties on the island (the UUP and DUP refused to attend, and Sinn Féin was excluded because of its support for violence). For many years, the basic assumption of Irish nationalists had been that a united Ireland was the only possible solution to the Northern Ireland problem. However, the Forum Report, published in May 1984, set out all the options which ought to be open for discussion. These included the traditional 'unitary' Irish state – although few observers saw this as a realistic possibility. More interestingly, the report outlined proposals for joint authority over Northern Ireland by Britain and the Republic, and for forms of a federal or confederate state. Although all the Forum's main options were dismissed rather peremptorily by the UK government soon after their publication, they served as an opening agenda for serious discussion.

First fruit was the Anglo-Irish Agreement of November 1985 which, as already noted, gave the Irish government an entitlement to be consulted on a wide range of Northern Ireland affairs. While diehard nationalists were angered at the associated formal recognition by Dublin of Northern Ireland's status within the UK, moderate nationalist opinion was strongly in favour: after more than sixty years the Unionist veto on progress appeared to have been removed. Unionists, on the other hand, were shocked and dismayed at the involvement of the 'foreign' Irish government in the internal affairs of Northern Ireland. Their anger eventually led to street protests, strikes and civil disobedience.

Because of this, progress thereafter was painfully slow, and it was not until April 1991 that the first effort at talks involving all Northern Ireland politicians (except Sinn Féin) and the British and Irish governments got off the ground. Although they ended without any agreement, there was general acceptance that there were 'three strands' – internal, North–South, and British–Irish – to be attended to if progress was to be made in creating a new future for Northern Ireland. In the meantime, Sinn Féin was engaged in a major re-think of its position, marked most signally by the re-opening of previously inconclusive talks with the leader of the SDLP. Though most observers expected little to come of this dialogue, John Hume of the SDLP and Gerry Adams of Sinn Féin did eventually arrive at a common position. This was put directly to the Irish government, and was the principal influence on a statement by the Minister for Foreign Affairs, in October 1993, of six democratic principles upon which a settlement in Northern Ireland ought to be based.

> They were: the people of Ireland, north and south, should freely determine their future; this could be expressed in new structures arising out of the three stranded relationship; there could be no change in Northern Ireland's status without freely-given majority

> consent; this could be withheld . . . the consent principle would be
> written into the Irish constitution; a place would be found at the
> negotiating table for [Sinn Féin] once the IRA had renounced vio-
> lence.[9]

Next, incorporating all of this, came the 'Downing Street
Declaration' of December 1993, signed by the British Prime
Minister and the Taoiseach. It also spelled out for the third time
in as many years that the British government had no 'selfish
strategic or economic interest in Northern Ireland'. The object
of this declaration was essentially to assist Sinn Féin in persuading the IRA that there was no longer, if there ever had been,
any justification for the use of other than democratic methods
in pursuit of republican political aims. It took until 31 August
1994 for the IRA to be convinced that negotiations might be
productive, and that a ceasefire should thus be called; but even
then the IRA refused categorically to declare that the ceasefire
was permanent. Soon after, the UVF and UDA also announced
ceasefires, conditional upon the maintenance of that of the
IRA.

The most important effect (after some hesitation on the part of
the British government about the 'permanence' of the cessation
of violence) was to bring Sinn Féin, the PUP and UDP into direct
contact with the British and Irish governments for the first time.
Sinn Féin and the loyalists also took part in a new 'Forum for
Peace and Reconciliation' set up by the Irish government,
intended to promote 'agreement and trust between both traditions in Ireland'. Previous British and Irish broadcasting bans on
paramilitaries and their political associates had also been lifted
by this stage, permitting leading figures like Adams access to the
public airwaves for the first time for many years.

Support from abroad, especially from the United States, for
what was now being called the 'peace process' was soon forth-
coming also; British troops were off the streets for the first
time for almost a quarter of a century; and in February 1995
the British and Irish governments issued their 'Framework'
documents setting out the parameters within which all-party
negotiations might take place. However, the issue of the

de-commissioning of paramilitary weapons proved to be a major stumbling block. The polar positions were, on the one hand, that Sinn Féin, the UDP and the PUP could not possibly take part in talks for so long as their paramilitary associates continued to hold arms – and could thus return to violence if they were not satisfied with the progress being made, or did not approve of the outcome of negotiations. On the other hand, the IRA, UVF and UDA simply refused to countenance any suggestion of a surrender of weapons until negotiations were complete.

In an effort to resolve the impasse, a team headed by former US Senator George Mitchell was invited to rule on the question. The 'Mitchell Principles' incorporated a compromise on the weapons issue, by proposing that 'de-commissioning talks' run in parallel with the substantive negotiations. The British government was not immediately in favour of this, and in what was claimed by some to be a diversionary tactic, accepted a Unionist demand that there be elections for membership of a 'Peace Forum', from which the negotiating teams for the main talks would also be selected. Sinn Féin and the SDLP saw no need for an election, and were frustrated by what they considered to be another British delaying tactic.

The significance of the IRA's refusal to declare its ceasefire permanent became all too apparent when a bomb exploded at Canary Wharf in London in March 1996, killing two people. This was followed by several other IRA actions against economic targets in Britain, as well as a mortar assault on a British Army base in Germany. The justification offered by the IRA for these attacks was British government and Unionist insincerity and prevarication, and the failure to set a date for the commencement of all-party talks.

Sinn Féin refused to condemn the IRA's resumption of violence, and was immediately excluded from further contacts with ministers of both governments. In the hope of achieving a restoration of the IRA ceasefire, however, London and Dublin agreed to set the opening of all-party negotiations for 10 June. But this was not sufficient to convince the IRA that the talks would be productive; and Sinn Féin was refused entry despite its assertion that this was a denial of the new mandate which its increased vote in the Forum election had demonstrated.

At the time of writing the talks have made only minimal progress; and the elected Peace Forum has devoted much of its time to procedural wrangles. The resumption of IRA violence which took up most press attention between March and mid-summer was briefly superseded in its news value by the opening of the 1996 'marching season'. Plainly against the wishes of the inhabitants, two important marches by the Orange Order were forced through Catholic areas and, in the worst communal violence for many years, widespread rioting and arson took place in both republican and loyalist areas. Although some compromises on the routing of parades were later reached, the British government was persuaded to set up a commission to look at the whole issue of contentious parades and demonstrations.

Just as dispiriting for those concerned to see political progress, a bomb wrecked an important tourist hotel in the Northern Ireland lakeland area of County Fermanagh. This was the first major action within Northern Ireland itself since the IRA's ceasefire broke, and there was general relief when it was credited to a republican splinter group. That relief was to be short lived. In October the IRA scored a major military success for itself, but dealt its Sinn Féin colleagues a serious political blow, by setting off two large car bombs inside the British Army's Northern Ireland Headquarters. Despite this provocation, the loyalist ceasefires held – but only by a thread.

## Notes

1 For early evidence of official concern, see, *Disturbances in Northern Ireland: Report of the Commission Appointed by the Governor of Northern Ireland*, Belfast: HMSO, 1969 (The Cameron Report). For an overview, see R. Cormack and R. Osborne (eds), *Religion, Education and Employment: Aspects of Equal Opportunity in Northern Ireland*, Belfast: Appletree, 1983.

2 The definitive story of the Northern Ireland civil rights movement can be found in B. Purdie, *Politics on the Streets*, Belfast: Blackstaff, 1990.

3 For an insight into the more extreme religious objections to a unitary Irish state, see P. O'Malley, *The Uncivil War: Ireland Today*, Belfast: Blackstaff, 1983.

4 Quoted in P. Buckland, *The Factory of Grievances: Devolved Government in Northern Ireland 1922-1939*, Dublin: Gill & Macmillan, 1979, p. 72.

5 D. Fell, 'Building a better economy', *TSB Economic and Business Review*, Vol. 1, No. 3, pp. 22-5, 1986.

6 B. Rowthorn, 'Northern Ireland: an economy in crisis', in P. Teague (ed.), *Beyond the Rhetoric: Politics, the Economy and Social Policy in Northern Ireland*, London: Lawrence & Wishart, 1987, p. 118.

7 See D. Hamilton. 'Industrial development', in N. Collins (ed), *Political Issues in Ireland Today*, Manchester: Manchester University Press, 1994.

8 M. Connolly and C. Knox, 'Recent political difficulties of local government in Northern Ireland', *Policy and Politics*, Vol. 16, No. 2, pp. 89-97, 1988.

9 P. Arthur and K. Jeffery, *Northern Ireland since 1968*, Oxford: Blackwell, (2nd Edition), 1996.

## Further reading

P. Arthur, *Government and Politics of Northern Ireland*, Harlow: Longman, 1987 (2nd edition).

M. Connolly, *Politics and Policy-making in Northern Ireland*, Hemel Hempstead: Philip Allen, 1990.

J. McGarry and B. O'Leary, *The Future of Northern Ireland*, Oxford: Clarendon Press, 1990.

J. Whyte, *Interpreting Northern Ireland*, Oxford: Oxford University Press, 1991.

# 8

# External relations

Ireland's place in the world economic order (as discussed in Chapter 1) influences its relations with other countries to a very great degree. Countries with which Ireland has significant trading relations are obviously the object of much government and private attention. Indeed, the establishment of Ireland's embassies, consulates and missions is guided in large part by considerations of trade. Other factors are also important: the pattern of Irish migration in this and previous generations; the spread of Irish missionary efforts; and the desire to forge a distinctive Irish foreign policy. In this chapter, the range of Ireland's relations with other countries is outlined, giving special attention to Britain, the USA, the EU, and the United Nations.

A feature of Irish foreign policy which marks it off from that of Britain or America is its neutrality. Both these countries are parts of the North Atlantic Treaty Organisation (NATO), an alliance formed after the Second World War to resist the threat of Soviet expansion. Most members of NATO had been parties to the war, and so too had most its counterparts in the Warsaw Pact – the Soviet bloc's equivalent of NATO. Ireland, however, remained neutral, and has maintained this stance ever since. Although neutrality had been a recurring theme in nationalist thinking for some time, the initial decision was almost entirely driven by the state of Anglo-Irish relations: the Irish government saw involvement in an alliance which included the United Kingdom as incompatible with the claim that Northern Ireland was part of the national territory. While the original decision was an essentially pragmatic one, however, neutrality has come to be seen by many people as an enduring assertion of the independence of the Irish State. There have, on the other hand, been calls in some quarters recently for a review of the policy, especially since the EU's Maastricht Treaty established the concept of a Common Foreign and Security Policy (CFSP; on which see more below).

## Relations with Britain

Ireland's relations with Britain are fashioned by a range of inter-related factors. The relationship is complex, involved and multi-faceted: the Republic is the only country with which the UK has a land border; many thousands of Irish citizens live in Britain (but have never been considered foreigners); for many professional, cultural, sporting and other social purposes, the two islands are treated jointly; British companies have invested readily in Ireland; Britain takes approximately one-quarter of Irish exports; Ireland is Britain's seventh largest export market; and even though Ireland became a republic in 1948, it has retained the favoured status usually enjoyed only by countries of the British Commonwealth. And yet, as we have seen, Northern Ireland is an important issue in both countries; it sometimes intrudes a jarring note into the development of policy, economic activity and social exchange that would otherwise have been expected to progress harmoniously.

The relations between Ireland and Britain are conditioned by a number of asymmetries of power. Britain is a large, highly developed state, which, while no longer the great and utterly self-confident power it once was, participates much more centrally than Ireland in world affairs. The British political leadership continues to see its international role as a significant one – in relation to world trade, military matters (including nuclear deterrence), scientific research and cultural endeavour. British diplomats, military personnel and business people are actively engaged in almost every major theatre of world affairs, through treaty obligations, vestiges of colonial responsibilities and economic self-interest.

Many small countries with powerful neighbours find it difficult to come to terms with their relatively minor place in the larger world's view. In Ireland's case, this difficulty is intensified by its former position in the British Empire. Some observers have argued that many components of Irish foreign policy arise purely from the need to assert the nation's status as an independent actor on a wider stage. As a consequence, Ireland pursues an active foreign policy on issues of no immediate material advantage to itself; often, though not contrivedly, it takes a contrary view to the UK on such issues.

For Ireland, nationalism is the dominant ideology. It binds diverse individuals into 'a people', acts as a motive for economic, cultural and sporting achievement, and provides a source of genuine pride and sympathy. The nation has become the highest affiliation and obligation of the individual, and through it a significant part of personal identity is formed. For some Irish people, however, much of the definition of that identity is found in contra-distinction to a British identity. National achievement is frequently measured relative to Britain, and to do better than England in particular is sufficient to define success. This attitude is inevitably reflected in matters of public policy. Issues are defined in nationalist terms very readily, and injustices, insults, ingratitude or ungraciousness to any one Irish person by 'the British' (in whatever form) is regarded as an injury to all. British politicians and bureaucrats are often insensitive to Irish nationalism; while they may treat other groups equally cavalierly, in Ireland such treatment is often seen as evidence of British antagonism, disrespect or disinterest.

Relations between Britain and Ireland are further complicated by the degree of attention each pays to the other. In Britain, domestic Irish politics (or at least that portion not relating directly to Northern Ireland) get similar coverage in the media to that given to the politics of France or Germany – sometimes less. By contrast, not only does the Irish media devote considerable space to British affairs, but British television and newspapers are freely and widely available. The reverse is not true. The Irish public is thus more aware of, and informed about, events in Britain than about events in any other country with which Ireland has dealings. This high level of British media penetration is reinforced by the ready movement of Irish people to and from Britain, for business and social reasons. Moreover, the easy communications between Ireland and Britain help solidify the generally favourable image of British people in Ireland.

These friendly attitudes do not extend, however, to the British government and 'Establishment'. Images of British institutions, as opposed to individuals, are mediated by the predominant nationalistic historical interpretation of the role of the British in denying Ireland's independence. As a result, Irish public policy to Britain has, until recently, been officially cautious, occasionally suspicious and always watchful. Since the Anglo-Irish Agreement in 1985, however, senior politicians and public officials enjoy useful, regular and friendly relations with their British counterparts. The two governments now work very closely on Northern Ireland policy, and this cooperation has had an impact in other areas. Symbolic of the improvement in relations was the visit of Prince Charles to the Republic and the state visit of President Robinson to Britain in 1996. It remains to be said that policy ideas, public inquiries, official reports and legislation originating in Britain remain amongst the most pervasive and persuasive outside influences on Irish politics today.

### Relations with the USA

Remarkably, Irish political relations with the USA also have much to do with Anglo-Irish relations. The USA, with its substantial ethnic Irish community, has often been considered as a potentially powerful ally in arguments with Britain over Northern Ireland. Such an outlook is ironic in that British politicians have since 1945 laid great stress on their 'special relationship' with America.

The attitudes of Irish Americans, particularly those who idetify emotionally with Ireland, are heavily tutored by their forefathers' experience. This was of rural Ireland under British political and landlord rule, and of America as a hopeful new home for poor emigrants. For Irish Americans who have not prospered, Britain remains a *bête noire*; and even among those who have enjoyed social and economic success in the USA, old images remain important. Yet many Irish Americans do not have any sustained, personal and direct experience of Ireland, and their ethnic sentiment, money and influence have often been used in ways that Irish governments find very unhelpful. As a result, much of Ireland's considerable diplomatic effort in the USA has been directed towards 're- educating' Irish-American opinion – opinion that has often been more intensely anti-British than domestic opinion.

Relations with the USA have been markedly assisted in recent years by the active involvement of 'The Friends of Ireland', a group of Democratic and Republican congressmen and senators strongly influenced by contacts with John Hume of the SDLP. The Friends have worked closely with Irish diplomats to help in the dissemination of the Irish government's case for peaceful reform in Northern Ireland. However, other Irish-American groups – such as Noraid (a registered IRA fund-raising body in the USA), the Irish National Caucus (which seeks to publicise the wrongs suffered by Catholics in Northern Ireland) and an *ad hoc* congressional committee on Ireland – together press forward a more republican interpretation of events in Northern Ireland.

Irish political influence on American policy has traditionally been greater in the legislature than in the executive branch, however. While it is no longer important whether the Republicans or the Democrats hold the Presidency, there are some barriers to Irish influence. Britain's sway in the State Department (the American department of foreign affairs) and the Department of Defense has always been sufficient to counter any unwelcome Irish manoeuvre. Irish neutrality during the Second World War, as unpopular in the United States as it was in the United Kingdom, has faded as a contentious issue, but Britain's centrality to American intelligence-gathering and other military involvement continues to be crucial. Further, the extensive economic and financial links between the USA and Britain are a significant factor in ensuring that the two countries' relations remain politically harmonious.

For all that, under the 1992-96 Clinton administration the politics of the Northern Ireland question received much greater presidential attention than ever before. Clinton showed a close personal interest in the problem, and members of his personal staff were actively involved in promoting peace initiatives of various kinds. The President took a major risk (by some accounts, against State Department advice) in permitting the leader of Sinn Féin to make a high-profile trip to the USA in early 1995, soon after the IRA and UVF/UDA ceasefires had been called. In November 1995 the President demonstrated his own commitment to the quest for peace by visiting Belfast, Derry and Dublin, in each of which cities he was warmly received. Though the UK remains more significant as an influence on American foreign policy, Irish voices are being heard more sympathetically than in the past.

On the whole, then, Irish-American relations are close, and usually become contentious only when British interests are at issue. They are likely to improve further if Ireland continues to be an attractive location for American investment. In addition to that, some 40 million Americans claim Irish origin; and while recent large-scale emigration effectively ended in the mid-1960s, many young Irish people continue to seek employment in the USA. Ireland thus retains important resources of goodwill, sentimental attachment and mutual economic self-interest in the USA.

### Relations within the European Union

Ireland's entry to what is now called the European Union, in 1973, was heralded by many nationalist-mined people as a chance to lessen decisively the influence of Britain on Irish life. It has indeed had a major impact, and Irish enthusiasm for Europe remains high. For a small state with a relatively open economy, participation in the Union has meant great economic opportunities and unusual political influence. When Ireland holds the presidency of Europe (as it did in the second half of 1996) Irish ministers play a more significant role on the world stage. At the same time, leaders of the Irish business community and senior public servants have seen the European Union as an opportunity to develop their talents in a wider setting. There has of course been some resistance to the EU, from groups who are concerned about the loss of Irish sovereignty; but overall, Ireland sees itself as an approving, active, enthusiastic and cooperative Union member.

Not least among the reasons for this is that since accession to the EU, Ireland has received considerable financial transfers from Union funds. Indeed, as late as the mid-1990s approximately 8 per cent of the government's current budget came from Brussels – funding which Irish officials have been vigorous and assiduous in gaining. To a significant extent, therefore, public policy in Ireland is EU-led – in that some programmes and projects are given priority principally because EU funding is available for them.

Arguably the major recent development within the EU was the creation in 1992 of the 'Single Market' which, virtually at a stroke, eliminated almost all the barriers to trade between member states. Trade with EU states has been a critical factor in Ireland's impressive economic growth and healthy surplus in the balance of payments. In preparation for 1992, the EU provided considerable assistance to the poorer parts of the Union, which brought the net transfers to Ireland since accession to around IR£20 billion. Europe also provided earmarked funding for economic development in border areas from which both parts of Ireland benefited.

Ireland's interests in Brussels are, like those of all member states, looked after by the country's Permanent Representation. This is a body akin to an embassy, which services important EU committees, the main one being COREPER: the Committee of Permanent Representatives of member states. In addition, Irish ministers and officials attend numerous EU meetings, ranging from the weekly management meeting to regulate certain farm commodities to those of the European Council itself. As was seen in Chapter 2, EU directives and regulations have considerable impact on domestic policies, often in areas where Irish thinking was previously underdeveloped.

The EU has developed politically since the original Treaty of Rome. The Treaty on European Union – the 'Maastricht Treaty' – came into force in November 1993. It provides for further economic and monetary unity between EU states and calls for the development of a Common Foreign and Security Policy. The Treaty was endorsed in Ireland by a referendum. It nevertheless represents a significant political challenge for Ireland – all the more so since the EU is likely to enlarge in the next decade to include several further nations in eastern and southern Europe. The impetus for enlargement comes from the security and economic interests of several current member states, most notably Germany. For Ireland, by contrast, enlargement may be costly in the longer term, because the institutional arrangements and financial benefits of the EU will have to change to take account of the new members and their needs.

For this reason a process of reviewing the EU Treaties, called the Intergovernmental Conference (IGC), began in March 1996. It is likely that nation states, especially the smaller ones such as Ireland, will have to accept a decline in their political independence as a price for greater European integration. National governments will have to accept more majority voting than is currently the case, presenting the possibility of having to abide by decisions with which they disagree. Further, more power will probably be given to the European Parliament, in which the Republic has only 15 of the 626 members. In an effort to pre-empt one of the other likely changes, Ireland has declared that it will not relinquish its right to nominate a member of the European Commission.

The Maastricht Treaty also aims to create a Common Foreign and Security Policy (CFSP). This ambition developed out of the experience of, firstly, European Political Cooperation (EPC), and secondly, the Western European Union (WEU). For twenty-two years under the EPC, all EU member states sought to coordinate their foreign policy. The EPC was not particularly constraining on member states, but it did allow some mutual cooperation on a number of occasions: during the upheavals in Afghanistan; concerning NATO's deployment of nuclear weapons; through the period of the collapse of the Soviet Union; and following the reunification of Germany. CFSP extends the EPC approach but, crucially for Ireland, looks towards a common defence policy.

The WEU already has a specific brief to deal with the military defence of Europe. The organisation includes all EU member states except Ireland, Austria, Denmark, Finland and Sweden – although these five countries have observer status. Under the Maastricht Treaty, however, the WEU is considered – for the first time – to be a part of the development of the EU. Furthermore, the WEU's own Treaty expires in 1998. Important questions will thus arise for Ireland and the IGC about defence policy for the future. Irish policy-makers have been keen to stress the distinction between 'security policy' and 'defence'. So if a majority of EU states wish to push beyond the Common Foreign and *Security* Policy towards a common *defence* policy, Ireland's traditional neutrality might be very difficult to retain.

Needless to say, there has begun to be debate in Ireland on this question. Opponents of neutrality say that Ireland should not attempt to hold back the development of a common EU defence policy. Playing a part in defending Europe against attack is, it is argued, a moral obligation on all those countries which would benefit from any agreed defence arrangements; moreover, other member states will grow impatient with Ireland's stance. Those who favour maintaining neutrality point to the advantages to Europe, and even to the rest of the world, of having at least one neutral member of the Union. The debate on neutrality has not been fully developed as yet, but is sure to become more intense as the 1990s move to a close. Meanwhile, Ireland has said it will cooperate with the WEU on certain types of peace keeping and humanitarian tasks; and the Fine Gael–Labour–Democratic Left government which took office in December 1994 felt it necessary to declare that the policy of neutrality would only be changed by a referendum.

The most pressing decision for Ireland in its relations with the EU is whether to become part of the Economic and Monetary Union (EMU) scheduled to be in place at the turn of the century. The EMU would involve a common currency and an EU central bank. To prepare for these developments, member states have to achieve certain monetary objectives. Ireland seems likely to meet the criteria and, in that sense, be ready to join. The critical unknown is whether the UK will wish to remain outside EMU. Thus, Ireland faces a great dilemma in relation to its major trading partner, Britain and, it follows, to Northern Ireland. As well as the prospect of an EMU/non-EMU border in Ireland, there is the serious danger that a devalued sterling would make Irish goods uncompetitive in their major market. On the other hand, EMU membership would bring important political and economic benefits. Ireland would enjoy lower interest rates, inflation and transaction (money exchange) costs. It would also give all the EMU countries a general economic boost. More fundamentally, Ireland would remain a part of the inner circle of European states.

## Relations with the United Nations

Ireland's activist and enthusiastic stance in relation to international organisations like the UN began in the 1920s and 1930s. The Free State's membership of the League of Nations was an important assertion of nationhood. De Valera, in particular, ensured that Ireland's pacific voice was heard in the 1930s, when Italian and German military policies were disturbing the world order. Until the mid-1950s, Ireland was excluded from the League's effective successor, the United Nations, because of a Soviet veto. However, it was again a de Valera government that brought Ireland back into membership, in 1957 – signalling an activist stance on contentious issues such as China's representation at the UN, arms control and disarmament.

In both the League and the UN, Ireland has been a constant advocate of giving maximum authority to the world body in settling disputes. Despite neutrality, for example, Ireland allowed US planes bound for the 1990 war with Iraq to refuel at Shannon Airport, because the American action had UN authority. Ireland is also strongly committed to UN peace-keeping and has sent troops to the Congo, Zaire, Cyprus, Lebanon, Sinai and the Iran–Iraq border. A source of much national satisfaction is that between 1958 and the mid-1990s, more than 42,000 Irish soldiers served with the UN in peace-keeping and other humanitarian tasks.

## Other external commitments

As we noted in Chapter 2, Ireland has another important European commitment, outside the EU. The European Convention for the Protection of Human Rights and Fundamental Freedoms (1950) is one of the most important of a large number of international declarations of rights made since 1945. In contrast with the United Nations' Universal Declaration of Human Rights (1947), and the subsequent UN charters of rights, the European Convention has an important element of collective enforcement (see also Chapter 5).

Since the late 1950s, Ireland has been a member of several other major international organisations: the International Monetary Fund; the International Bank for Reconstruction and Development; the International Finance Corporation; and the International Development Association. Ireland is a founder member of the Organisation for Economic Cooperation and Development, which, together with its affiliates, helps the twenty-four member countries' governments with the formulation of economic and social policy. Its reports are often a focus of debate in Ireland, because of their wide comparative analysis and authoritative style.

In common with other countries, Ireland uses its assistance to developing countries as part of its foreign policy. Ireland spent in the region of IR£106 million in 1996 (0.3 per cent of GNP) on development assistance to Third World countries. This represents at least a doubling since 1992, although there are frequent complaints that this falls seriously short of the UN target of 0.7

per cent of GNP. Approximately 40 per cent of total aid is expended on bilateral assistance (direct Irish aid to developing countries), and the rest is given to international organisations to support their development activities. Over 60 per cent of bilateral aid is spent in projects in Ireland's six priority sub-Saharan countries: Ethiopia, Uganda, Lesotho, Tanzania, Zambia and the Sudan. The largest sectors for expenditure are agricultural and rural development, education and training. The aim of the aid is to reduce poverty, foster democracy, respond to disasters and contribute to building civil society and social solidarity. It is possible that Mozambique will be added to the list of priority countries, as Ireland's aid budget increases.

## Conclusions

As in many other countries, external relations are often discussed in Ireland in terms of sovereignty. The idea that a nation state should have power and control over its own future is very strongly held. In reality, Ireland is as constrained in foreign affairs as it is in other areas of policy by its position in the world economy. Additionally, it is influenced by the same tight network of international obligations, organisations and agreements as all other modern countries. Indeed, while the Republic of Ireland now has all the symbols of independence, the level of its interdependence with the rest of the world has never been greater. Nation states no longer have complete and actual control over the direction of policy in their own territory, even if they do so formally. There are clearly difficulties, therefore, in analysing external relations in terms of purely formal sovereignty.

To begin with, the world economic system serves to limit the autonomy of national governments. In Chapter 1, we examined Ireland's place in the international division of labour and saw that it competed with other semi-peripheral countries for international investment. A key role in this global system is played by multinational companies for which national boundaries are less important than comparative costs and opportunities. For such companies, technological advances in communications and transportation have eroded the relevance of independent national economic policies. Ireland's foreign policy is thus aimed in part at protecting the Irish economy from the vagaries of the world economic order – by cooperating with other countries for the coordination of policy. To a degree, therefore, sovereignty is now about collective action by states.

The demands of mutual defence erode sovereignty also. Irish foreign policy may soon have to come to terms with greater European cooperation on defence, with the obvious difficulties which this presents for neutrality. The pressure for a European defence policy is itself a product of the changes within the hegemonic power blocs that dominate world politics. Most of Ireland's EU partners are part of an alliance which limits them as autonomous military actors. NATO nations do retain the capacity for independent military action, but they also recognise the reality of collective security. Although not all NATO countries participate fully, the existence of an integrated supranational command structure ensures that, in certain military crises, 'national armies' will operate under supreme allied command. Given that its partners have qualified their national sovereignty in the name of collective defence, it is likely that this is the model which will be used to shape any specifically EU security arrangements. More important, however, are the doubts about the continuation of American commitment to the defence of Europe, about the East–West negotiations on conventional forces in Europe, and about the effects of political ferment in the former Communist countries in eastern Europe. These will present western Europe with new political and military choices, for which Ireland may have to assume some responsibility.

The rapidly changing context in which Ireland arranges its external relations involves the world economic order, international treaties, other countries' arrangements for collective defence, international law and the EU. All of these may appear to undermine Ireland's independence of action – its sovereignty. In fact, many of the obligations and constraints which arise from all this represent an enhancement of Ireland's potential as an economic and political actor. The EU, in particular, protects the national economy, the environment and human potential of its citizens. It certainly allows Ireland to make a more significant impact on world developments – on world politics today – than it otherwise could.

## Further reading

P. Arthur, *Aspirations and Assertions: Britain, Ireland and the Northern Ireland Problem*, London: Routledge, 1991.

M. Holmes, N. Rees and B. Whelan, *The Poor Relation: Irish Foreign Policy and the Third World*, Dublin: Gill Macmillan, 1993.

P. Keatinge, *A Singular Stance: Irish Neutrality in the 1980s*, Dublin: Institute of Public Administration, 1984.

P. Keatinge (ed.), *Ireland and EC Membership Evaluated*, London: Frances Pinter, 1991.

D. Scott, *Ireland and the IGC*, Dublin: Institute for European Affairs, 1996.

# Index